DUBLINESE

DUBLINESE
KNOW WHAT I MEAN?

B E R N A R D   S H A R E

The Collins Press

Published in 2006 by
The Collins Press
West Link Park
Doughcloyne
Wilton
Cork

British Library Cataloguing in Publication Data
Share, Bernard
  Dublinese : know what I mean?
  1. English language - Dialects - Ireland - Dublin
  2. English language - Ireland - Dublin
  I. Title
  427.9'41835

ISBN-10: 1905172079
ISBN-13: 978-1-905-172078

Typesetting: Dominic Carroll, Ardfield, Co. Cork
Printed in Malta

CONTENTS

FOREWORD

For one to fully understand Dubliners, one must learn their language — or, rather, languages. Within this formerly compact and intimate city, there existed a range of socially and environmentally defined idioms rejoicing in their own way of saying — or not saying — things, of coming to terms with different perspectives on daily occurrences. Under the impact of social, political and demographic change, these idioms have, over the generations, undergone modification and mutation and have been complemented by the new accents and colloquialisms of today. The result, as we look at it from the point of view of the early twenty-first century, is a living and distinctive utterance that draws both on the bilingual richness of the native past and the many external influences to which Dublin, successively a regional, national, colonial, independent and international capital, has been subjected.

Through centuries of settlement, conquest and change, the everyday language of the city has thus acquired its own accent, vocabulary and idiom. This book explores and illustrates these characteristics, quoting extensively from all levels of usage and drawing upon a comprehensive range of sources. This exploration ranges from the historical sources of Dublinese to colloquial place names, and the language of transport from sedan chair to Luas, from profanity and vulgarity to commerce and day-to-day living. An extensive literary range — from Swift, Sheridan and Goldsmith to Joyce, Beckett, O'Casey and Roddy Doyle — is covered. But the book draws equally on the language of Joe and Josephine Soap and their co-citizens from many walks of life. All have enriched the idiom of a city which, to coin a blasphemy, is in essence the word made flesh.

An excursion through Dublinese rather than a dictionary, this book lays no claim to be fully comprehensive — but then no study of a living language, dictionary or otherwise, ever can be. Since I completed the second edition of *Slanguage — A Dictionary of Slang and Colloquial English in Ireland* in 2003, I have filled a substantial notebook with new words, and new uses for old words, and there is no sense in which such a process can ever be complete. That is part of the fascination, and the frustration: as soon as the last proof is passed, a word or phrase lurking in the inner recesses of the daily newspaper or half-overheard on the 46A bus clamours for attention. There is every reason to believe, therefore, that readers of this book will feel compelled to complain about what is *not* here, but I hope that they will find it comprehensive and wide-ranging enough to map in some detail the verbal landscape of a city which in so many respects is changing before our eyes — and in so many respects remaining very much its unique and inimitable self.

1

FROM THE DANES
TO TODAY

And as for you yourself, my dear Nancy, I hope I shall never
have any more of your London English; none of your winegars,
your weals, your vindors, your toastesses and your stone post-
esses: but let me have our own good plain, old Irish English,
which I insist upon is better than all the English English that
ever coquets and coxcombs brought into the land.

Charles Macklin, *The True-Born Irishman*

Charles Macklin, actor and playwright, whose original name
may or may not have been Melaghlin or MacLoughlin and
who may or may not have been born in Donegal, wrote his comedy
around 1793. His patriotic and protesting hero, Murrough
O'Dogherty, is burdened with a socially ambitious wife who, after a
visit to London, scorns everything Irish from dress to diphthongs in
favour of the superior English model, prompting her long-suffer-
ing husband to respond in the manner quoted above.

We may assume that O'Dogherty's advocacy of 'good, plain
old Irish English' refers to that spoken in Dublin, or at least in the
Pale, since at the turn of the century, Connacht, Munster and
large areas of north Leinster were still predominantly Irish-
speaking, with only Dublin, Wicklow, Kildare, Carlow and parts of

Wexford substantially anglophone. O'Dogherty was aggressively proud of his Gaelic heritage, reacting strongly to his wife's anglicising her name to Diggerty (a foretaste of worse things to come): 'Why,' he protested, 'they have no such name in all England as O'Dogherty — nor as any of our fine sounding Milesian names — what are your Jones and your Stones, your Rice and your Price, your Heads and your Foots, and Hands, and your Wills, Hills and Mills, and Sands, and a parcel of little pimping names that a man would not pick out of the street, compared to the O'Donovans, O'Callaghans, O'Sullivans, O'Brallaghans, O'Shaghnesseys, O'Flahertys, O'Gallaghers and O'Dogherty's ...' Nevertheless, O'Dogherty clearly belonged to the anglicised landed classes, and his speech was that of urban Dublin. His conviction of the superiority of his Irish English was to be replicated by many patriotic advocates over the following century or more, with increasingly specific reference to the English of Dublin. Thus in James Joyce's *Portrait of the Artist as a Young Man* (1916):

> Is that called a tundish in Ireland? asked the dean. I never heard the word in my life.
> It is called a tundish in Lower Drumcondra, said Stephen, where they speak the best English.[1]

PURE FANTASY

The language of Lower Drumcondra was to alter somewhat in subsequent years, as will be observed; but to the succession of visiting firemen who, from the Elizabethan Edmund Spenser onwards, recorded their impressions of the country, and particularly of the capital, the linguistic claim was not infrequently the cause of some amusement. As Thomas Cromwell, a dissenting minister, put it in 1820:

An idea is very prevalent among the inhabitants [of Dublin] that the English language is spoken in greater purity in their city than in any other throughout the British Empire. An opinion this, at which the travelled Englishman, whose recollection probably will furnish him with an instance of the same harmless nationality in the good citizens of Edinburgh, must be constrained to smile ...

It was an idea that was slow to go away. Post-Joyce, for example, Oliver St John Gogarty quotes a conversation with the learned Dr Tyrrell of Trinity in which the latter, having cited two negative Greek enclitics (words joined so closely to the previous word as to lose their normal emphasis) continues

Seemingly Dublin has a more negative asseveration. It is at its best in an example. 'Picnic' [they had been discussing picnics] reminds me:
'Are you coming to the picnic, Mrs Murphy?'
'Picnic, ME NECK! Look at Mary's belly since the last picnic.'[2]

And Gogarty adds: 'The presence of this third enclitic "me neck!" proves that Dublin still uses the English language as emphatically as the Elizabethans could.'

OUL' BAGS

Some few decades later, however, Gene Kerrigan could lament, in his memoir of 1950s Dublin, the loss of something of this distinctive emphasis.

That generation though receiving a minimal education, seemed on average to have a better facility with words — better handwriting even — than we do and to use language more precisely. A word such as ACCOUTREMENTS, meaning bags

3

and baggage, was commonplace. Today, we'd settle for 'I'm picking up my stuff.' If someone used the word PERAMBULATE or WHEREWITHAL in everyday conversation (and someone might) there was no need to explain it.[3]

But according to the writer and film-maker Jim Sheridan, quoted by Anne Simpson, Dublin has not entirely lost it. 'The English,' he reflects, 'insist that Dubliners speak the best English in the world. "They don't but they may speak the most entertaining English. They speak with hyperbole and circumlocution which the English speak directly"'.[4] Or as Vincent Caprani expressed it:

When the English robbed our language
And they gave us theirs instead,
They gave us leave to cheat them
In the things we left unsaid;
When they robbed us of our claymores
And thought our pikes absurd
We fashioned brand-new weapons
With each odd, new-fangled word.[5]

THE MEERE IRISH

The history and development of the English language in Ireland are both complex and contentious — particularly so in Dublin. Though the city was, by the eighteenth century, as the poet Louis MacNeice described it, the 'Augustan capital of a Gaelic nation', the Irish language was still the vernacular in one or two quarters, notably the Liberties and an area behind the North Quays, as late as 1815. As early as 1577, however, the Oxford-educated Dubliner Richard Stanihurst, in his contribution to Holinshed's *Chronicles*, was alleging of the English settlers in Wexford

that they have so acquainted themselves with the Irish, as

4

they have made a mingle-mangle or gallimufry of both languages and have in such medley or checkerwise to crabbedly
jumble them both together, as commonly they speak neither
good English nor good Irish.[6]

And whatever about Wexford, he could foresee the 'mingle
mangle' conquering the seat of colonial power: 'It is not expedi-
ent,' he said, 'that the Irish tongue should be so gaggled in the
English pale ...' However, it was, even then, a case of shutting
the stable door, for, anticipating Mrs Diggerty by a couple of
centuries, he tells of the aspirations of 'the inhabitants of the
English pale, upon their first repair into England, to learn their
English in three or four days, as though they had bought at
Chester a grote's worth of English, and so packed up the rest to be
carried after them to London ...' Hiberno-English, it would
appear, was already flourishing in Dublin. And the incomprehen-
sion was working both ways. A nobleman, according to
Stanihurst, 'being very glad that upon his first coming to Ireland,
he understood so many words, told one of his familiar friends
that he stood in very great hope to become shortly a well-
spoken man in the Irish, supposing that the blunt people had
prattled Irish, all the while they jangled English.'

Apart from a few enduring place names (such as Howth,
Dalkey and Leixlip), it is difficult to identify very many elements of
a Scandinavian input into the Dublin diction of today. However, as
early as AD 856, according to Kenneth Jackson, 'within a generation of the first settlements, we begin to hear of a mixed population of Norse Irish, the Gall-Ghoídhil, who were evidently
recognised as distinct from both the Irish and from the
Scandinavians proper.'[7] The invading Anglo-Normans of the
twelfth century brought with them both English and Norman
French, so that the Dublin of about 1200 must have been, linguistically speaking, a very confusing city. In the subsequent centuries, English was to fight a losing battle with Irish throughout

the country, except in the fortified towns and in Dublin in particular. As the English traveller Fynes Morrison wrote of the late
1500s:

> the meere Irish disdayned to learn or speake the English
> tongue, yea the English Irish and the very Cittizens (excepting
> those of Dublin where the lord Deputy resides) though they
> could speake English as well as wee, yet commonly speake
> Irish among themselves ...[8]

On this evidence, Dublin, in contrast with the rest of the country,
must have remained to a greater or lesser extent anglophone
throughout its post-Norman history, though with what form of
English at any given period is open to speculation. Fingal, north of
Dublin, 'a little territory', as Fynes Morrison saw it, 'as it were the
garner [granary] of the Kingdom' preserved a unique dialect,
related to that of Forth and Bargy in Wexford, until about 1800.
(Now, with its own county administration, it is reasserting its
geographical identity, even if its linguistic singularity has vanished beyond recall.) Whatever changes the imposed language
may have undergone through the centuries of conquest, in the
view of Alan Bliss, 'it can be demonstrated that the English of
Ireland at the present day is descended from a sub-standard,
partly dialectal variety of English, of a type current about the
middle of the seventeenth century'.[9]

VOWEL PLAY

The 'coquets and coxcombs', in O'Dogherty's phrase, who
brought English into Ireland from 1169 onward were as varied as
were their versions of the language. Once having delivered it to the
initially unwelcoming Irish-speaking natives, however, these
latter were left for the most part to make of it what they could.
The number of Mrs Diggertys who were to bring back the latest

phonetic fashions from London was constrained by both distance and the attendant difficulties of passage, so that Hiberno-English developed its own vocabulary, syntax and pronunciation, all profoundly influenced by Irish. Thus Macklin makes fun of Mrs Diggerty's aping of alien London speech:

> *Mrs Dig*: Brother, I am veestly glad to see you.
> *Counsel*: Welcome from England, sister.
> *Mrs Dig*: I am imminsely obligated to you, brother.[10]

Meanwhile, the Dublin actor, theatre manager, lexicographer and elocutionist Thomas Sheridan, father of the dramatist Richard Brinsley, offered a professional assessment in *A Course of Lectures on Elocution* (1762):

> the gentlemen of Ireland, for instance, differ from those of England, chiefly in two of the sounds belonging to the vowels /ä/ and /ë/ sounded by them /ā/ and /ē/ and even with regard to those also, not always, but only in certain words ... Thus the words patron, matron, are pronounced by them p/ā/tron, m/ā/tron, the *a* being sounded as it is in father; fever, sea, please, are pronounced like favour, say, plays. They soon become conscious of this diversity of sound, and not knowing exactly in what words it is used, in order to imitate the English pronunciation, they adopt the sound /ee/ in all words without distinction; instead of great they say greet, for occasion occeesion, days, dees &c.[11]

THE VOICE OF THE LOBSTER

The characteristics of Hiberno-English here under review and exemplified in the diction of Mrs Diggerty represent, of course, those of the Ascendancy planters rather than the native Irish. However, as English became the second, and ultimately the first, language of the latter, its dissemination was given added impetus through the emergence in Penal times of the hedge-schoolmasters eager to impart their knowledge of the new language but lacking the grounding and the educational apparatus of textbooks and dictionaries (though the latter-day 'Bolton Books', cheap, mass-produced readers, were, to some extent, to fill the gap). These autodidacts read widely but often with an imperfect grasp of the new language, and in passing it on to their pupils created their own version of it, based on the model of the still widely-spoken Gaelic vernacular. One consequence of this was the emergence of something that Dubliner Richard Brinsley Sheridan (*The Rivals*, 1775) was to immortalise in the person of Mrs Malaprop and for which he had surely found his model in contemporary Hiberno-English usage: 'Ah, few gentlemen, nowadays, know how to value the INEFFECTUAL qualities in a woman!'[12] Samuel A. Ossory Fitzpatrick records an eighteenth-century performance of *Othello* in Smock Alley in which the actor in the leading role, attempting the lines

> Oh, my Lord! Beware of jealousy;
> It is a green-eyed monster.

blithely substituted 'It is a green-eyed LOBSTER.'[13]

INSANITARY SPECTRES

Among the examples of malapropism, as it came to be known, noted some two centuries later by the lexicographer P.W. Joyce, was: 'What had you for dinner today?' 'Oh, I had bacon and goose and several other COMBUSTIBLES.'[14] According to Alan J. Bliss:

> This tendency can be observed in any part of Ireland but it is especially common in Dublin, and O'Casey makes extensive use of it in his plays: FORMULARIES for 'formalities', for instance,

or DECLIVITY for 'proclivity'. Some of these are, no doubt, just slips, but some of them recur, and may be due to an erroneous interpretation by some hedge schoolmaster.[15]

The malapropism is, happily, still with us in Dublin diction, which can still refer to one of the city's oldest charities as the Sick and INDIGNANT Roomkeepers' Society (properly perpetuated in the Sick & Indigent Song club, the reincarnation of a Dublin-based roots band). Within recent memory an advertisement in a Dublin paper for the London Jurys Hotel promised that 'The elegance of this unique Luytens landmark building, the grand scale of its reception and meeting areas and the sensitivity of its restoration, guarantee an experience to be RELINQUISHED and slowly savoured'. And Dominic Behan's Mr Clancy:

'D'YE KNOW WHAT I'M GOIN' TO TELL YEH? If any of that crowd pay their rent two weeks runnin' the polis is up to know where they got it. An' of course, that's not the worst of it.'
'No?'
'Not by half. There's the IDOLATERS ...'
'Idolaters?'
That's right ... a fancy name for fancy men who sleeps with other people's wives ...'[16]

In 1988, the City of Dublin declared itself to be 1,000 years old (even though available records go back a good deal earlier than 988). This millennial non-event was persistently referred to in certain quarters as THE ALUMINIUM YEAR. Less felicitous is the example that not infrequently appears in death notices, for example in a Dublin daily newspaper of February 2005:

SOAP (Joseph). (Melbourne and formerly Churchtown, Dublin) – February 1, 2005 following a brief illness, to the INEXPLICABLE grief of his wife ... [name and details changed].

KNOWING YOUR ONIONS

Among examples logged on the overheardindublin.com website were (April 2005): 'a neighbour of ours ... was complaining to my ma about kids hanging around at the side of her house. She asked my ma why the kids had to CORRUGATE outside her house all the time'; '... sure aren't all o' dem Italian fellas supposed to be hung like SCALLIONS.' On 18 October 2005, it was announced that 'Plans to convert the 130-year-old Lansdowne Road Stadium into a 50,000 all-seater "EPHEMERAL addition to the skyline of Dublin" have been unveiled'.[17] The report went on to quote, somewhat contradictorily, John Delaney of the Football Association of Ireland: 'What you want is permanence, you need a permanent home'. And what might be termed the reverse malapropism is also not unknown in contemporary usage. 'When I issued a simple instruction', an unworldly teacher complained to her staff-room colleagues in *The Irish Times* supplement, *Education Times,* 'the class erupted into a gross exhibition of loud, vulgar behaviour. I told that awful child, Karen, to stop MASTICATING and then all hell broke loose. I cannot understand why.'

COD É SIN?

While the above question addressed to the proprietor of a Dublin CHIPPER would be unlikely to elicit an informative response, any discussion of Hiberno-English must take into account the fact that traces of the Irish language will present themselves in various guises in everyday usage. Diarmuid Doyle has pointed to the use of the language amongst Irish holidaymakers abroad:

> Our cute Irish friends want to make some bitchy, smutty remarks about their colleagues, or maybe they just want to squeeze them out of the conversation. And so they start to talk *as Gaeilge*. "*Ní caithfeadh mé Luigi as an leaba is é ag ithe* TAYTOS". "*Féach ar na BAPS on that*".[18]

This defensive use of the language (it was employed for the same purpose by the Irish UN troops in the Lebanon until it was discovered that they were being overheard on the Israeli side by a number of emigrant Dublin Jews) is in sharp contrast to 'Irish language's unpopularity', which, in the view of Diarmuid Doyle, 'is rooted in the kind of MUCKSAVAGERY with which it is surrounded. It has become the international language of CUTE HOORISM ...'

TAKE TEN

Back in 1953, at the time of the TÓSTAL, a national festival designed to lure tourists, the actress Siobhán McKenna 'counselled everyone who can speak Irish to make a point of speaking it for at least ten minutes every day. She was convinced that if this were done in Ireland it would be a big advance'.[19] Her suggestion prompted the following response from Myles na gCopaleen: 'Can you imagine the mentality of people who put the Irish language on the same level as bending exercises in the morning?'

> *You'll have to excuse me, lads* (throws down poker hand). *I'll be away for ten minutes.*
> Where are you going?
> *Out into the garden.*
> But it's raining and it's nearly midnight. What are you going out there for?
> *To speak Irish for ten minutes.*[20]

TÁ SÉ MAHOGANY GASPIPE

In the late 1940s and early 1950s, a right-wing republican organisation calling itself *Aiseirí* plastered Dublin with posters demanding *BÁS DON BÉARLA – TEANGA* BHASIL BROOKE. Brooke, then Northern Ireland prime minister, was subsequently to be ennobled as Lord Brookeborough. At the same time, those crossing

Westmoreland Street through the scanty traffic were invited to TREASNA ANNSEO, pausing en route to admire a couple of men leaning on shovels behind an equally monolingual placard stating *FIR AG OBAIR*. While this is not the place to discuss the wider exposure of the Irish language, it must be noted that, whatever about its current evidence in public places and everyday urban communication, Irish words and phrases contribute to a greater or lesser extent to the richness of the Hiberno-English idiom.

In March 2005, John Creedon's RTÉ radio programme conducted a search for the nation's favourite Irish words. Of the shortlist of ten[21] only two, *fáilte,* a welcome, and *aisling,* a vision but also a common girl's name, could be said to have any currency among Dublin English speakers, and the former would owe its familiarity largely to the long-term existence of Bord Fáilte, the state tourism organisation, and the ritual greeting, *Céad míle fáilte.* Other Irish-named state-sponsored bodies have given rise to imaginative colloquial variations. According to Stephen Collins 'Another pivotal development in getting [1987] economic strategy right was the establishment of the Expenditure Review Committee, which became known as AN BORD SNIP',[22] while Jim Dunne recalled:

> when Bewley's [café] was in one of its frequent financial meltdowns, a politician – Garret FitzGerald, I think – proposed it should be taken into State ownership. This idea was roundly and rightly attacked by the DOHENY AND NESBITT SCHOOL OF ECONOMICS as AN BORD BUN.[23]

The ad hoc academic body referred to was a political talking-shop benefiting from the hospitality of a traditional Dublin pub. Another such establishment 'was also the scene of many an informal political meeting and members of Garret FitzGerald's think-tank – informally known as the NATIONAL FONDLERS (< national handlers, aka spin doctors) – were regularly to be spotted in Dobbins' back-room.[24]

The demise of Aer Rianta, one of the most venerable state bodies, and its reincarnation as the Dublin Airport Authority in 2005 served to highlight a virtual abandonment of the practice of naming public bodies in Irish (An Bord Báinne had earlier transmogrified itself into the Irish Dairy Board). Irreverent Dublin wit, however, continues to manifest itself in whatever language: 'There is really no end to the empire being bestowed on Michael Somers in the National Treasury Agency, aka AUNTIE MAC', commented the *Sunday Business Post:* '... Now the role of the final part of the NTMA — the National Development Finance Agency – is being expanded. Set up a couple of years ago to advise on raising money to fund state building projects, it was immediately christened UNCLE NED'.[25]

AS GAEILGE

'We never heard a word of Irish spoken except on St Patrick's Day', C.S. Andrews recalled of his Dublin childhood in the second decade of the twentieth century: 'although Gaelic words persisted in the common speech of the people much more than they do today. Words like *flaithiúlach, gob, amadán, a stór, óinseach, strap* and *praiscín* were quite usual';[26] but the regular occurrence of unreconstructed Irish words and expressions in today's otherwise multilingual Dublin is, to put it mildly, relatively limited. Thus an anecdote from the website overheardindublin, quoted by Shane Hegarty[27]:

> I was standing at a bus stop on O'Connell Street. There were two girls beside me talking Irish to each other. Next thing you know, two local Dubliners walk by and hear the two girls talking. One of the Dubliners looks at the two girls and says 'Hey, fuck off back to yer own country.'

Hegarty's comment: 'It's about as insightful a look in the capital, and the country, as you can get from four lines.' Otherwise you might hear *gúna*, for example: 'Gawping at one female contestant's outfit, he [Derek Mooney] observed: "That GUNA, or what you're wearing of it, looks fantastic, heh, heh, heh".'[28] Likewise FLAHOOLACH, <Ir. *flaithiúlach*, lavish, generous, and, more in the contemporary idiom, *sneachta,* snow (cocaine) — others will be referenced in context.

With rare exceptions, however, it cannot be asserted with any conviction that these usages are exclusive to, or typical of Dublinese, though perhaps Fergus Cassidy's skit on the Drumcondra speech of Taoiseach Bertie Ahern (a favourite target — see Chapter 3) might be admitted:

1. The Dubs v Man Utd in CROKER. Who'd win? Posted by P. Ness on 19 April @ 10.23pm.
2. Are ya tryin' to wreck me CEANN [head] or wha? I'll take the answer to me grave! Posted by B. Ahern on 19 April @ 10.55pm.[29]

And from Arthur Reardon's 2005 musical, *Improbable Frequency*: 'His name is Muldoon and he might sing a tune/So let's have some CIÚNAS [quiet] please!'

AN INCH PAST THE CIRCULAR ROAD

When Budapest became the capital of Hungary in 1873 with the unification of Pest and Buda, it entered upon an era of expansion and change of character which, according to István Bart,

> cut Budapest off from the rest of the country, which regarded it as a 'sinful city' and resented it, too, for it attracted the country's talent and money to itself like a magnet (and indeed, those whose forebears had lived in Budapest, like themselves, are still in the minority) ...[30]

The phenomenon of one major centre dominating a city or state is not uncommon, as in the case of Sydney in New South Wales, Cairo in Egypt, Reykjavik in Iceland, and many others, giving rise to the rural/urban dichotomy about which the Spanish priest Antonio de Guevara wrote in his *Menosprecio de Corte y Alabanza de Aldea* ('Contempt of the Court and Praise of the Village') in 1539 but which has manifested itself in many other times and places both before and since, originating, perhaps, with Aesop's fable of the Court Mouse and the Country Mouse, with the verdict nearly always in favour of the calm of the country as against the corruption of the court. The Irish example, which has of late become a cause of serious demographic concern, has its roots in the pattern of colonisation which created the Pale, an enclave which, though it was to prove to be porous both politically and linguistically, was to set the speech patterns of Dubliners, together with their attitude to the rural population at large.

COUNTRY CUTE

The city dweller's pretence of contempt for a person from rural parts is reflected in such words as BOGMAN, BOGTROTTER, COUNTRY MOWHAWK, the Swiftian YAHOO, or even BALUBA ... The term of ultimate abuse for an ignorant person is CULCHIE ...[31]

Gerry O'Flaherty's 1975 listing, though many elements would be recognised by the citizen of today, is a lesson in the constant mutability of language usage. BALUBA passed into popular speech as a result of the experience of the Irish troops serving in the Congo in the 1960s on their first UN mission, in which they suffered serious casualties. It is questionable, however, if it ever became an exclusively Dublin term applied to CULCHIES but was perhaps a more generalised term of abuse. Anyone jumping to the conclusion that its day is past, however, will find it living again under another guise in Chapter 5 and might also consider the case of GUBU, an acronym coined in 1982 by Conor Cruise O'Brien, making use of some of the adjectives (grotesque, unbelievable, bizarre, unprecedented) employed by the then Taoiseach Charles Haughey with particular reference to a political scandal involving the Attorney General. One might have been justified in assuming that it would have enjoyed a currency no longer than that of the scandal itself, but it was current as late as 2005 when a contributor to the RTÉ radio programme, *Tonight with Vincent Browne*, said of the Health Bill controversy then raging, 'it's one of these GUBU things' — an adjectival usage that will perhaps withstand the further test of time.

BOG STANDARD

Of the balance of O'Flaherty's snapshot of the 1970s, YAHOO, Jonathan Swift's contemptuous coinage in *Gulliver's Travels*, is now more readily encountered as the trade name of an internet portal; Mohawk (the name means 'man-eater' and was conferred on the North American nation of that name by one of its enemies) has probably succumbed to political correctness; but BOGMAN and BOGTROTTER, and their variations BOGGER, BOGGERMAN and, rarely, the pc BOG PERSONS) remain in the urban lexicon, together with BOGLAND: anywhere beyond the Pale. Whereas the terms denoting the rural dweller's perceived origins in the rural peatlands require no gloss, the term CULCHIE has for long been a cause of etymological challenge and counter-challenge. The popular favourite, and the one that would appear to carry the greatest authority, derives the term from the Mayo town of Kiltimagh (Ir. *Coillte Mach*) from when large numbers of men were transported to the Midlands, especially to the environs of Edenderry, Co. Offaly, to harvest essential turf during the Emergency (known elsewhere as the Second World War). Not everyone, however, is acquiescent in this etymology. Writing to

The Irish Times, Gearóid Ó Gabhláin insisted that 'This proud son of a Mayo man takes issue with those who claim the term "culchie" is derived from the name of the Mayo town of Kiltimagh. This would be equivalent to claiming that the term JACKEEN is derived from the Indonesian capital of Jakarta!'[32]

Be that as it may, while there have been many other speculative derivations[33] of greater or lesser plausibility, the word remains vigorously current as a generalised denigration of anyone not fortunate enough to be, either by birth or osmosis, a DUB. 'GAA's north-south divide for Dublin bears marks of classic culchie plot' was the heading on a Frank McDonald article[34] on the occasion of a proposal by the country's leading (and, many would allege, culchie-ridden) sporting authority (The Gaelic Association, aka THE GRAB-ALL ASSOCIATION, the governing body of the sport known to soccer-loving Dubs as BOGBALL) to carve up Dublin County horizontally to create two teams, or sets of teams, where hitherto the team had been defined by the county boundaries. Myles na gCopaleen, a blow-in Dub but absolved from real culchiedom by the fact that he hailed from County Tyrone — the Six Counties are by some sleight of hand exempted — popularised TURNIP-SNAGGERS as the epitome of the culchie ethos, with the implication that anyone falling into that category could not help but be TWO FOOT THICKER THAN BUTT BRIDGE, until relatively recently the last crossing of the Liffey before it spills into Dublin Bay.

HABEAS CORPO

Dublin county had, administratively speaking, ceased to exist in January 1994 when it was divided into four separate entities. Of these, the former Dublin Corporation, the much maligned CORPO, re-emerged as the Dublin City Council. So who, or what, is a Dub? In GAA terms, at least, the term continued to identify the football and hurling teams and their supporters; but writing in the autumn of 1995 in the week following Dublin's winning SAM (the Sam Maguire Cup) in the All-Ireland Football Final, Seamus Martin asserted:

> the very term 'Dubs' has an arrogant ring to it. When the people of other counties, or at least those who get to Croke Park for the semi-finals and finals, give vocal support to their team, they shout for their counties. 'Up Galway' 'Come on the Banner', '*Tír Eoghain Abú*' and even 'Up Down' ... Only Dublin fans replace the name of their county with that of a mythical race of beings.[35]

And the rest of the country, up for the match or otherwise, is not unresponsive to the pretensions of this privileged race. 'Can there be a capital in the world [more] disliked by the rest of its country than Dublin is by the rest of Ireland?' asked Martin. 'Can there be another country where the citizens of the capital look down so much on the inhabitants of the provinces? As a Dublinman, but certainly not a "Dub", I feel that our side is as much to blame as the other side.'

In the sporting context at least, the proposition was accorded some authenticity in Anto Byrne's *Diary of a Dublin Football Fan*: 'Today's de big day, wha? Second bite a de cherry again de sheepshaggers a Kildayer and Ine telling ye, if dee don't do de business today, Im never goin to see de Dubs again ... Ine never going ta see dat shower again if dee don't beat dem sheepshaggin' bastards.'[36] (It is only fair to point out, if in parenthesis, that the non-Dubs are well able to respond in kind. Discussing the 2005 Cork Film festival, Dermot Bolger observed that 'To the urbane sensibilities of Cork, I suspect that 'The Last Temptation' would only have been blasphemous if it established that Jesus Christ was from Dublin'.[37])

In this perennial confrontation of Pale and Province the colloquial vocabulary employed by both sides can be both accusative and self-defining. (There is only one word, according to Tom

Corkery[38] 'that can be mispronounced in the same way by both the countryman and the Jackeen. Offeecial, says the countryman, of his county manager. 'Offeecial', says the Jack, of his clerk in the Labour). 'People from other parts of Ireland refer to Dubliners as Jackeens or Gurriers' wrote Gerry O'Flaherty:

> Jackeen, in the city always meant a cunning, loud-mouthed ignorant youth: while Gurrier was a term of approbation . . . .
> In the [Nineteen] 30s and 40s to be Great Little Gurrier was to be a bosom friend, a fine fellow, a taproom companion: but today it has been debased and is the equivalent of a BOWSEY or a GOUGER.[39]

NOM DE GUERRE?

JACKEEN, according to P.W. Joyce – a Limerickman – is 'a nickname for a conceited Dubliner of the lower class'[40] and follows the common formation of an English word to which is added the Irish diminutive suffix *ín*, anglicised as –een (GIRLEEN, etc.). For Hugh Leonard, Brendan Behan was 'the greatest living example of that rare creature known as the DUBLIN JACKEEN: a being who is by tradition bawdy, witty, irresponsible, fiercely loyal, iconoclastic and withering, yet who is riddled with unexpected demarcation lines beyond which is perdition'.[41] GURRIER, randomly employed by both sides in the argument, is etymologically the most interesting and the most controversial, attracting, as in the parallel case of CULCHIE, its share of inspired guesses as well as scholastic hypotheses. The following is advanced by the distinguished lexicographer Diarmaid Ó Muirithe:

> I have heard people arguing about this word in pubs; I have heard it discussed on radio and television programmes, and many years ago the late Séamus Kelly tried to solve the problem of its provenance in 'An Irishman's Diary' in *The Irish*

Times. He was convinced that the word was borrowed from their French allies by Irish soldiers in the Great War, and that *gurrier* was simply the Dublin pronunciation of *guerrier.* Nay, nay, thrice nay![42]

He goes on to suggest a derivation from *gurrie,* an English dialect word meaning to growl like a dog – an etymology unlikely to appeal to native gurriers, let alone BOWLERS. P.W. Joyce[43] has *gurry,* a young pig (Irish *banbh* < bonham), though it would be wise not to make too much of that in true gurrier company. Safer, if perhaps even less convincing, might be the suggestion contained in a letter from Máirtín Mac Con Iomaire:

> For the last year, I have been amusing my friends with an anecdote based on Regina Sexton's contribution on GUR CAKE found in the *Oxford Companion to Food.* Gur cake is a type of fruit slice particularly associated with Dublin. It is made from stale cake, pastry or cuttings that were crumbed or mixed with raisins, mixed spice, caramel colouring and water, spread on a sheet of pastry, baked, covered in icing sugar and then cut into squares. Regina Sexton proposed that the term 'gurrier' was established in Dublin dialect, describing 'one who eats gur cake; a tough street urchin.'

Maybe, but it was far from any class of cake that many tough street urchins were reared.[44]

NOT ON THE LEVEL

In the context of the considerably less affluent and less danger-ous Dublin of the 1960s, Liam Ó Cunaigh offered an annotated list of less confrontational classes of Dubliners, beginning with HARD CHAWS who, he said 'differ from CHANCERS in so far as they will risk jail for love of their profession, whereas chancers always come away with a dividend ... MESSERS and LOUSERS you know. Wasters too. But I'm afraid you're not a true Dubliner until you belong to, or can recognise on sight, these other species', and he goes on to consider SKINS – 'usually decent, mellowing with the years to become DECENT OUL' SKINS, TICKETS – 'must be hard'; STEWMERS, GOMS and CASES:

> a hard case is a milder version of a hard chaw, though moving dangerously in that direction. He works on the floor of steel plants and factories and insists upon a regular stream of innocent apprentices, these he dispatches to the far end of the machine room, to ask Paddy English for a long wait (weight), or the loan of a size seven alcohol bubble for a spirit level.[45]

FULL MANY A JEM ...

The generic DUBLINMAN, according to Ó Cunaigh, 'will address another as JEM, which may he varied to JEMSER if the person referred to is not within their hearing: or JEMBO if he is a child'.[46] As Vincent Caprani records in *A Walk Around Dublin* (1992):

> One of my recent saunters down by the docks was enriched by a casual encounter with a square-jawed septuagenarian in a cloth cap and a blue gansey who (if I'd taken the trouble to ask his name) would, I feel, have inevitably answered 'Jem', or WHACKER or NEDSER.[47]

These and other metamorphoses of the Dubliner or Dublinman (Dublinwomen are an as yet undocumented species) used to be confined, by general assent, within the area bounded to the north and south by the Royal and Grand canals. Beyond was injun territory, or as the character Noel put it in Brendan Behan's *Moving Out*, a play dealing with an inner-city family exiled to the then new suburb of Crumlin: 'You little EEDGIT, you're as bad as my da. Anywhere an inch past the Circular Road and you think you're in Texas.'[48] Or, in the view of the Kerry writer Bryan MacMahon: 'To the average Dublin boy the land beyond the Red Cow, a famous inn near suburban Clondalkin, is *terra incognita*, where hefty, hairy Culchies ... armed with clubs clump around the bogs in search of well-behaved "gurriers" or city lads.'[49]

TIME AND TIDE

Whilst that mentality may persist, the city has in fact spread uncontrollably in all directions into the adjacent counties, and with it the language and to a lesser degree the mind-set of the capital, so that the Dublin accent is rapidly diluting and in many instances replacing the indigenous intonations of contiguous Meath, Kildare and Wicklow. Myles na gCopaleen, writing half a century ago and more, was prophetic:

> One hears a lot of talk about 'Greater Dublin' (most of it unau-thorised by me and therefore mischievous) but never a mention of the sticking-out corollary that, according as you increase Dublin, you diminish the rest of Ireland proportion-ately. This, of course, is a very serious matter. Some fine day the inhabitants of Leixlip will notice something unusual about the horizon and, sending forth scouts to investigate, will find it is Dublin. Dublin just down the road today. Tomorrow? The tide will have engulfed ancient Leixlip ... People will write letters addressed 'Main St. Leixlip, Dublin c.98.' and you will probably be able to get there on the 16 bus. People in Athlone will say "You saw what happened in Leixlip. They thought they were safe, that their unborn sons would never be Dublin men. *Hodie Leixlip, cras nobis.*[50]

And it has gone further than Myles ever imagined. 'One of these days,' prophesied Shane Hegarty in 2005, 'you'll arrive back from a fortnight in Lanzarote to find the entire island of Ireland hidden behind scaffolding ... A handful of men in high visibility jackets will be staring down a hole where Athlone used to be'.[51]

So where does that leave what we used to know as Dublin? No longer a county in an administrative context, but divided into rebellious Fingal (when they put up WELCOME TO CO. FINGAL signs they were vandalised, presumably by loyal Dubs) and South Dublin and Dún Laoghaire–Rathdown County Councils – perhaps the unimaginative choice of names was a feeble effort to prevent the latter two 'ridings' (in the true origin of the word as 'thirdings') also taking upon themselves a semblance of individual identity. There are new Dubliner commuting colonies in Mullingar, Gorey, Portlaoise (and, indeed, Athlone), and there will be even more before this is in print; and with them there has emerged what Dave Kenny, author of *The Little Buke of Dublin*, calls Culchie Dubs: 'these are Dubliners who have moved to other counties in Leinster. Some say you can't be a real Dub unless you live between the two canals'.[52] For the purposes of this enquiry we will continue to assume the old city, more or less within the canals, as the linguistic nucleus, *fons et origo*, even if one of the formative influences upon current Dublinese, the broadcasting stations of Radio Telefís Éireann, TV3 and sundry independents, for the most part do not fall within these limits. 'From swerve of shore to bend of bay . . .': James Joyce, triangulating the inflated Dublin of today, would have his work cut out.

2

THE WORD ON
THE STREETS

I was slumped in the back of a cab en route to the city centre
from the airport after a quick trip to London last week. The
cab swung down the quays past the much-vaunted IFSC
[International Financial Services Centre]. Nodding his head at
the development, the cabby sniffed, 'CANARY DWARF, WHA'?'

Lise Hand, *Sunday Tribune*, 3 October 2004

A vernacular map of the city would bear little resemblance to
the official products of the Ordnance Survey. The features,
streets and buildings of many cities have been nicknamed by
their citizens or interested others (Sydneysiders can probably still
be relied upon to bridle when they hear 'the Coathanger' applied
to their harbour bridge by Melbournians) but Dublin is particularly rich in an alternative nomenclature, almost exclusively
home-grown. And the nicknames have increasingly acquired a
habit of appearing almost before the building or monument
achieves completion, perhaps because this has in many cases
proved to be an interminably protracted process.

THE GAME OF THE NAME

On 8 March 1966, the pillar that had supported the statue of Admiral Lord Nelson for 157 years was blown up by a person or persons unknown. In *Ulysses*, James Joyce had recorded 'two old TRICKIES' who climb the Pillar 'and settle down on their striped petticoats, peering up at the statue of THE ONEHANDLED ADULTERER.' When, in the fullness of time, it was finally agreed that a replacement in the form of a monument of markedly slender proportions should occupy the by now long-vacant site, the letters pages of the newspapers were filled with suggestions for naming the SPIKE, as it was almost immediately labelled.[1] One somewhat uninspired suggestion, THE TAPER NEAR THE 'SCRAPER' (referring to the sixteen-storey Liberty Hall) echoed a pattern of rhyming nicknames which provoked the disapproval of John Moran:

> Of course the ubiquitous wags who regularly 'dub' new additions to the Dublin streetscapes with their vile rhyming doggerel have been at it again. THE JAB IN THE SLAB, THE LAMPSTAND IN CLAMPLAND, THE SPIKE IN THE DYKE and THE STILLETTO IN THE GHETTO are but a few of their base coinages ...'[2]

Previous targets of the rhyming 'ubiquitous wags' had included the trough-like monument containing an anomalous female figure and only recently removed from the shadow of the Spike, variously dubbed THE FLOOZIE IN THE JACUZZI, THE HOOR IN THE SEWER, THE VIAGRA FALLS, THE MOT IN THE POT, and perhaps most wittily THE BIDET MULLIGAN[3]).

Meanwhile, the cube-like Waterways building at the entrance to the Grand Canal was labelled THE BOX IN THE DOCKS. Journalist Brenda Power was intrigued by

> the misogynistic flavour of most of the side-splitting nick-names that we now employ to mock Dublin's civic furniture. Inoffensive Molly Malone is THE TART WITH THE CART [also THE DISH

WITH THE FISH] and the two gossiping shopping ladies at HA'PENNY BRIDGE are THE HAGS WITH THE BAGS ... Any visitor would be entitled to conclude that all of these ladies post a major affront to our national aesthetic sensibilities ... not only are we telling the world that we have a pitiful lack of confidence and pride in our national monuments, we are also betraying a dark and complex psycho-sexual unease over the prominence of strong female images that would have had old Freud rubbing his hands with glee.[4]

CAT FIGHT

The O'Connell Street monument, predictably, failed to meet its deadline of 1 January 2000, and the business of giving it a name was to return to public debate in 2003 when a completion date seemed finally in prospect. Anthony Glavin's proposal of MILLIGAN[5] seemed promising, even if the creator of the Goons, like Nelson, lacked any Dublin connection. Oliver McGrane ecumenically offered the PROD (see Chapter 4), while a suggestion to name it after Constance Markievicz assumed perhaps too much of the average citizen. This had already been made apparent by a comment in the *Mise Éire* column of *The Bell* under the heading *Cat-leen ni Houlihan!* on the inscription on her monument in St Stephen's Green:

Bean chalma chróda a throid I gcat ar son na hÉireann ... um Cháise im bliadhain an Tighearna a 1916.
Literal Translation:
A brave, valiant woman who fought in a cat for Ireland about cheese in the year of the Lord 1916.[6]

In the closing months of 2003, scarcely a day was to pass when *Irish Times* readers (and they were by no means alone) failed to propose new labels for an artefact, which, if still failing to rise to the occasion, by now appeared to have acquired the uninspiring official designation of The Spire. 'Surely we can come up with something that reflects our Irish culture?' complained Matt Doyle of the National Graves Association (as far as is known, nobody is buried underneath it). He went on to suggest AN CLAIDHEAMH SOLUIS (the sword of light), a tribute to Padraig Pearse and his brief tenure at the nearby General Post Office, a name which would certainly have come even less trippingly off the tongue than that of Madame Marckieviez. BRIAN BORU came into the reckoning, as did less serious attempts, among them THE POINTLESS POINT (echoing the average Dubliner's bemusement at the nature and purpose of the whole thing), and THE LONG FINGER (TO PUT ON THE LONG FINGER: to subject to inordinate procrastination). The latter's proponent, M.D. Kennedy, suggested that 'not only would it be an apt description, but it would serve as a permanent reminder of the interminable delays associated with virtually every public project, including the erection of the spire itself.'

WATER MUSIC

Happily, earlier dubbings of Dublin's public monuments had been a little more original. On 16 June 1904 Leopold Bloom passed the statue of Tom Moore (1857) in College Street: 'They did right to put him up over a urinal, MEETING OF THE WATERS.'[7] The likeness of Moore, by the undistinguished sculptor Christopher Moore (no relation), quickly became the target of parody-prone Dublin wit, ensuring that if the urinals are long gone, the nickname is still remembered:

'Twas not that somebody had placed on a slab
A heavy-cloaked gentleman calling a cab
And noting its number with pencil or quill,
Oh no! — it was something more hideous still.

Charles Stuart Parnell, or his effigy, stands at the north end of O'Connell Street, his outstretched hand pointing, most Dubliners will confirm, at Mooney's public house, in the spirit of the quotation on his plinth, 'thus far shalt thou go and no further'. Though he has apparently failed to acquire a facetious sobriquet (the UNCROWNED KING was a serious tribute), his name, according to the poet Austin Clarke, has nevertheless passed into colloquial usage.[8] Clarke quotes 'a priest from the Pro-Cathedral, who had questioned a young man about a girl he had seduced in a hallway. "What did you say she held?" "Me PARNELL, Father." "Your what?"' (James Joyce, for some reason, addressed his own procreative organ as ELLWOOD). Not far away, three figures representing Neptune, Wealth and Mercury stood above the portico of the Custom House until the building was burned in 1921. What was left of them was removed to a corner of the grounds where they were speedily identified by Dubliners as THE THREE STOOGES.

TÓSTAL LOSS

In the spring of 1953, the now superseded Dublin Corporation (known universally as THE CORPO) was moved to mark the inauguration of An Tóstal, an annual tourist-luring exercise which was to run for some years. 'I would like to record what happened the Tóstal in the town of Carlow', wrote Myles na gCopaleen[9]: 'They had a great week of it altogether with no less than Charles Lynch playing the piano. *Not one single stranger was in town!* Be that as it may, the Corpo had installed at the centre of O'Connell Bridge a plastic 'flame' surmounting a concrete trough (the enduring municipal fondness for troughs no doubt harks back to horse-drawn days) which, was not only generally vilified but attracted to itself the nickname of the TOMB OF THE UNKNOWN GURRIER. One Anthony Wilson, then a Trinity medical student, disposed of the 'flame' to the bottom of the Liffey, but the trough, spasmodically furnished with wilting flowers, lingered on. A complementary observation was recorded by Séamus Kelly, aka the columnist Quidnunc (who objected in print to a correspondent addressing him as 'Dear Pound-Now'), writing in *The Irish Times*:

> The scene was Burgh Quay. It was Thursday morning. Rainstorms and blizzards were sweeping Dublin. Two bedraggled men with watering-cans dismantled a folding ladder near one of the flower-bedecked Tóstal standards. As they prepared to move off, one of them shook the rain from his hat, looked sadly at the sky and said to his colleague: 'A WHALE OF A DAY to be out watherin' flowers!'[10]

The predilection for blowing up Dublin's statues, and with them, their acquired nicknames, goes back at least as far as 1836, when that of King Billy in College Green was demolished by gunpowder. Sir Hubert Gough was unseated from his horse in the Phoenix Park on 23 July 1957, as commemorated by Vincent Caprani:

> There are strange things done from twelve to one
> In the Hollow of PHAYNIX Park,
> There's maidens mobbed and gentlemen robbed
> In the bushes after dark;
> But the strangest of all within human recall
> Concerns the statue of Gough,
> 'Twas a terrible fact, and a most wicked act,
> For his BOLLIX they tried to blow off![11]

SI MONUMENTA REQUIRIS

Poor Field Marshal Viscount Gough was too far removed from general circulation to have acquired a pseudonymic identity. His sovereign, Victoria, sat outside Leinster House in solid bronze for 40 years from 1908 before being displaced and dispatched first to Kilmainham and subsequently to the more beneficent environment of constitutionally loyal Australia. Her ugly, 186-ton likeness was, during the period of her residence, known as IRELAND'S REVENGE. (On the occasion of her dethronement, *Dublin Opinion* carried a cartoon (August 1948) in which the be-scaffolded monarch is turning to address the passing Taoiseach: 'BEGOB, Éamon, there's great changes around here!') More recently, Edward Delaney's rugged monument to Wolfe Tone on St Stephen's Green (1967) was speedily identified as TONEHENGE, whilst his tribute to Thomas Davis in College Green (1966), featuring a fountain that worked intermittently, earned the sobriquet, after Davis' poem, URINATION ONCE AGAIN. The rhyming formula, however, was not abandoned: THE PRICK WITH THE STICK was applied to the statue of James Joyce in North Earl Street (1990); that of Oscar Wilde in Merrion Square is the QUARE ON THE SQUARE and the sitting image of the poet Patrick Kavanagh on the bank of his beloved Grand Canal (lined by trees which have been anecdotally described as MORE SINNED AGAINST THAN SINNING) was labelled — or libelled — the CRANK ON THE BANK This predictable mode of rhyming vulgarity does not yet appear to have run its course. Writing of the erection of a statue to the musician Phil Lynott, Rosita Boland observed that 'it will only be a matter of time until Dubliners find a nickname for the most recent addition to their streets. Given that it's going to be placed outside a bar, any takers for the DUB BY THE PUB?'[12] No.

Outside this tired formula and somewhat more original was the baptising of the newly refurbished Government Buildings (formerly the College of Science) in Merrion Street as the CHAS MAHAL (< Charles J. Haughey, the then Taoiseach who was responsible for the upgrading); though this was, in fact, a pale variation on the Taj Micheál, the nickname acquired by the new Galway Cathedral (< Micheál Browne, then Bishop of Galway and the force behind its construction in 1966). In recent times, however, Dublin's most talked-about public edifice was one which, to date, has not yet been built, not to mention named: the sports complex at the far side of the Phoenix Park, the brain-child of the incumbent Taoiseach, Bertie Ahern. 'Like the promise of an ice factory in a Latin American village in a magic realist novel.' wrote Tom Humphries, 'the BERTIE BOWL hovers in our imaginations ... Already, before its fate is decided, the Bertie Bowl has come to exist like a relic from another era.'[13]

ÁRAS WAYS

The Phoenix Park, otherwise FEENO, is as good a place as any from which to begin an excursion into the city's language of nick-names. Within its boundaries lie several features which have attracted a colloquial identity. Éamonn MacThomáis wrote

> We, in Dublin, haven't even a lake unless you allow me to mention the DOG POND up in the Park. Now every real Dubliner knows the Dog Pond, but the country fella up working in the Ordnance Survey Depot making out his map of the Phoenix Park, what does he call it? The Citadel Pond.[14]

The FIFTEEN ACRES is an open area of some 200 acres statute measure. Áras an Uachtaráin, the former Vice-Regal Lodge, which on its becoming the residence, first of the Governor-General and subsequently of the President of Ireland, saw its popular nomenclature undergo a series of modifications from UNCLE TIM'S CABIN (< Tim Healy, first Governor-General, 1922) and thus christened by Oliver St. John Gogarty, to HYDE PARK (< Douglas Hyde, first President, 1938) to ARAS AN LEPRECHAUN (< diminutive stature of Seán T. O'Kelly, president 1945). From 1990 to 1997 it was the official residence of ROBBO, aka President Mary Robinson. Vincent Browne wrote of a promotional trip by her successor, Mary McAleese, 'On to Chile a few days later, more plugging of the Celtic Tiger, at enormous length (3,042 words). Robbo would have made some reference to the Pinochet years, MACA, not a word.'[15]

DEAD OR ALIVE

Close to the ÁRAS, as it is generally referred to, are the Zoological Gardens, in popular speech boasting the extra (epenthetic) vowel (A-ZOO), a feature of a certain social and geographical Dublin accent. Another animal repository, on the other hand, has acquired no added vowels. 'A cross between a taxidermist's workshop and a hunter's trophy room,' wrote Mary Mulvihill,[16] 'it [the Natural History Museum] is affectionately known to generations of Dubliners as THE DEAD ZOO.' During the Emergency (1939–45), the fuel shortage prompted greatly increased activity on the midland turf-bogs. According to Alex Findlater,

> Twenty-nine new wooden canal barges were ordered and the stock conveyed to Phoenix Park and built into enormous ridges on both sides of the main thoroughfare — now named the NEW BOG ROAD.[17]

The 'Old Bog Road' was the title of Teresa Brayton's sentimental ballad of 1868. (This massive resource of fuel was, however, in no way the responsibility of a TURF ACCOUNTANT, the long-running euphemism for the profession of bookmaker, the city premises of which, devoid of any visible calorific presence, mystified many a youngster.) The massive Wellington Monument, now effectively ignored and forgotten, was known disparagingly in its heyday as the BIG MILESTONE. Sarah Bridge, close to the Park entrance, 'from the peculiar elegance of its proportions', wrote Samuel Lewis, 'has been distinguished by the name of THE IRISH RIALTO'.[18] The name is perpetuated in a modest suburb and its LUAS stop.

The Phoenix Park lies on the northern bank of the River Liffey, but its nature and relative remoteness from the city centre set it apart from a pervasive, and historically pugnacious, north–south divide. Dublin shares this rooted dichotomy with many other cities divided by rivers: Budapest, Drogheda, Sydney, and the Molvanian capital, Lutenblag, which encapsulates the common attitude of mutual contempt in that it was 'originally made up of two towns, *Luten* ('place of many hills') and *Blag* ('municipal tip').[19] Even the eventual bridges – across the Danube, Boyne or Sydney harbour – usually fail to induce a union of hearts and minds. As the character Chris puts it in Brendan Behan's *Moving Out*: 'That's the Dublin people all over. Never a good word for one another, from one street to the next. When I was going with your father, the people over our side of the city said to me, "Chris Coyle, don't say you're getting married into that clique over there. Sure in that quarter they eat their dead".'[20] The division is as much psychological as physical – perhaps more so. As Gareth Jones, a graphic designer living on the southern river bank, concluded: 'It's amazing that everyone divides Dublin by the Liffey, because it's a tiny thing.'[21]

NORTH CIDER, SOUTH CIDER

The Bulmer's ad on the Loop Line bridge (in spring 2006) epitomises this rivalry, the roots of which can be traced at least as far back as the often bloody confrontations between the Liberty Boys and the Ormond Boys, southside and northside respectively, at the close of the eighteenth century. According to John Edward Walsh, 'Among the lower orders, a feud and deadly hostility had grown up between the LIBERTY BOYS, or tailors and weavers of the Coombe, and the ORMOND BOYS, or butchers who lived in Ormond market, on Ormond quay, which caused frequent conflicts.'[22] One of these was celebrated in the street song, 'De May-Bush' (see Chapter 3), rich in the Dublin slang of the day, which celebrates an encounter in which, in accordance with the tradition on 1 May, the Liberty boys cut down a bush which had been set up in

Smithfield by the opposing faction. Bill Durham (the name was a common corruption of Dermot) sat astride the bush as it was carried back to be set up, singing 'as sweet as a TRUSH' with 'his pipe in his MUSH [mouth]' — quite a feat in itself. Having, however, succumbed to the effects of the celebrations he 'was now in his FLEA-PARK, taking a snore', when he heard the Liberty boys passing his door:

> Den over his shoulders his flesh-bag he TREW,
>> Ri rigidi ri dum dee,
> And out of the CHIMBLEY his faulchion he drew,
> And, mad as a hatter, down May-lane he flew,
>> Ri rigidi dum de!

But he was too late: 'BE DE HOKEY, de glory of Smidfield in gone!' Bill vowed revenge:

> In de slaughtering season we'll tip 'em a SWEAT ... [Sweat: a
>> prick with a sword]
> We'll wallop a mosey down Mead-street in tune,
> And we won't leave a weaver alive on de Coombe;
> But we'll rip up his TRIPE-BAG, and burn his loom ... [tripe-bag:
>> belly].

The historic Liberties themselves are, at the time of writing, apparently under threat of being dismally and disastrously re-christened SoHo (complete with the obsequious capital H). As MacDara Ferris observed: 'I do not want my great grandfather, Pádraig Breathnach, to be rebranded as the last silk weaver of So Ho. Let's not lose another piece of Dubllin, even if it is only a name, to so-called progress.[23]

US AND THEM

Though the sectarian basis for this particular trans-Liffey confrontation has long since succumbed to the realities of history, it has been transmuted itself into an expression of mutual aversion and suspicion which is only partly humorous. And there is no neutral ground. Tom Matthews' *Artoon*[24] depicts an orchestral conductor under the banner of the Smetana Festival announcing, 'Yes, I intend to conduct his best-known work on either the north or the south of the Liffey', prompting the comment from a bystander. 'He doesn't know which side his bride is bartered on'.

Fiona Looney made a brave attempt to be even-handed in the matter in cataloguing both 'Reasons why I hate the southside of Dublin' balanced by '10 things I hate about the northside of Dublin and the people who reside there'.[25] Included in the former category were 'The lack of knowledge of anywhere north of the Liffey; the accent and the way everything is "like, soooo, okay, ROIGHT; the ivory tower snobbery, masked by a pseudo liberal, trendy front'. Among the faults she found with the northside were: 'the incomprehensible accent, only identifiable as English by the frequent use of F and C words; everyone's name ends in "o" (MICKO, WHACKO, JOHNNO) ... or "er" (MICKSER, WHACKER, JOXER); the popularity of handbag-robbing'. And if she is careful to appear dispassionate (a seriously impossible position for any real Dubliner), her pseudonymous colleague Ross O'Carroll Kelly, in his regular column in the same newspaper, leaves little doubt as to where he stands: 'Why did God invent orgasms? So northsiders would know when to stop riding'[26] — a fair specimen of a type of joke common in the vernacular.

NO COFFEE IN CASTLEKNOCK

To O'Carroll Kelly the whole of the northside is a *terra incognita,* inhabited by CREAMERS, which he labels KNACKERAGUA. But the term KNACKER, originally a buyer of old worn-out horses for slaughter (a meaning which survived in Dublin into the twentieth century in the firm of 'O'Keeffe's the Knackers' on Thomas Street), had developed connotations which transcend the divide. 'Many Irish people grew up not realising that the word knacker was a hated word to describe the travelling community,' wrote Anne Marie Hourihane: 'In expensive schools on the southside of Dublin today, the word knacker is used to describe anyone not wearing the right trainers — in other words anyone with less money than the speaker.'[27] From the northsiders' point of view, to Conor Goodman and his friends, the southside 'was a vague territory where some people's cousins lived, all of them mollycoddled children with affected enunciation who ate funny food.'[28] And as for those, like himself, who crossed the boundaries: 'the DALKEY DESPERADO is a person who has been priced out of their native southern suburb, yet still shops in the Merrion Centre, banks in Killiney and spends Friday nights in Finnegans of Dalkey, before taking a cab home to Phibsborough.' Goodman has his own shot at a definition:

> ... just what the two terms meant was no clearer to me than when I was a child. (How baffling it must be for non-Dubliners.) 'Southside' seems to refer primarily to Dublin 4 and the plush suburbs to the west and south. North Dublin is comparatively vast, but the 'northside' tag is most often applied to the inner suburbs. In the middle-class outer districts, it means that you occasionally adopt a bogus salt-of-the-earth accent to discuss 'the gee-gees' and say things like 'Far from mochaccino lattes we was RARED'. It's the CASTLEKNOCK COMMONER phenomenon.

Senan Molony had a try at delineating the accepted vernacular dichotomy in terms of comparative branches of the fast-food chain, McDonald's:

DUBLIN (North): 'Howaarya. Worral it be? Z'aspeshul on deh-deh luksis'. [Hello, what'll it be? There's a special on the de luxe quarter pounders.]

DUBLIN (South): 'Hoi, hoysitt gohing. Oym yur survur fur today. Wuttud you lurk?' [Hello, I'm your server for today. What would you like?][29]

DUBLIN DECODED

But the north–south dichotomy has outgrown itself in other respects as well: Tallaght, a southside suburb which, since the coming of the LUAS trams in 2004, has undergone a major image change, is nevertheless still considered by O'Carroll Kelly (a view that would be shared by not a few other southsiders) as another Knackeragua:

JP sidles up to Eddie Jordan, ROYSH, and asks him why he doesn't just sack his mechanics, roysh, and hire a bunch of HEADS from TALLAFORNIA instead. And of course Eddie's like, 'Why would I want to do that?' and JP goes, 'Well, it takes your mechanics eight seconds to get the wheels off a car. Your average SKANGBALL from D24 can do it in six.'[30]

The 'D24' is significant. Pending the introduction of postal codes, the Dublin *arrondissement* (as in Paris) is identified with a sub-stantial degree of social snobbery. Thus, some years ago, the inhabitants of an area contiguous to the fashionable and expen-sive Dublin 6 (aka Rathmines/Rathgar) insisted on the inconsistent designation '6W' rather than accept some other far-out even number (even numbers southside, odd numbers northside); and DUBLIN 4 is recognised, and has become a synonym of, the haven of the affluent and the socially ambitious. 'Over the years the letters column of *The Irish Times* has been full of attacks on the so-called Dublin mindset', Tom Doorley wrote in the same paper:

As to what this actually means, I'm a bit hazy, but I think I'm right in saying that it includes a shameless indifference to headage payments, a somewhat half-hearted approach to the restoration of the Irish language, a tendency not to be frightened of sushi and a preference for mainstream political parties over the ... er ... Provisional movement.[31]

Many of these attributes found their focus and *raison d'être* in the DOHENY & NESBITT SCHOOL OF ECONOMICS, located in a hospitable pub on Lower Baggot Street which, in the 1980s and for some time thereafter, attracted the professional blathering classes.

This image, or self-image, however, is somewhat compromised by the fact that Dublin 4 includes, on its eastern extremity, a suburb still some social distance from the ABC1 category beloved of advertising agencies, the former fishing village of RAYTOWN, now known as Ringsend. As Vincent Caprani elucidates:

Expert opinions differ as to the official title of this ancient part of Dublin ... Alternative suggestions claim it as *Rinn Abhainn*, 'the point of the river', or that its name may have arisen from the large blocks of stone into which rings of iron were inserted for mooring vessels, and that such rings 'ended' at this point on the Liffey's southern wall. In his *Story of Dublin* D.A. Chart humorously infers that this latter is 'a typical IRISH BULL, as a 'ring' has neither a 'beginning' nor an 'end'."[32]

It has been proposed, only half in jest, that Ringsend should be relegated to a newly minted *cordon sanitaire* of Dublin 4E, a suggestion not unlikely to elicit the response of a RINGSEND UPPER-CUT — a kick in the groin.

BULL'S LOOKS

While so-called Irish bulls are not specifically of Dublin or even Irish origin,[33] they have a long and colourful association with the city, the outstanding contributor to the genre being Dublin-born Sir Boyle Roche (1743–1807), contemporaneously known as BOYLE BALDERDASH, who, speaking of the Act of Union in 1799 in the Irish House of Commons, stated that 'I would have the two sisters [Britain and Ireland] embrace like one brother' and to whom is attributed the frequently-quoted rhetorical question 'Why should we put ourselves out of our way to do anything for posterity, for what has posterity done for us?' He went on to explain that by posterity he did not at all mean our ancestors, but those who were to come immediately after them.

That Sir Boyle's posterity, freed from this ingenious time-warp, has not altogether forsaken the bull is evidenced by a recent newspaper report of 'a potent smell' emanating from Dublin's Grand Canal Basin. Dead fish were floating on the surface and, *The Irish Times* account stated, 'the lough [*sic*] was opened to allow live fish escape into FRESH SEAWATER.'[34] And, as befits the city's newly emerging multicultural complexion, its mala-propisms appear to have developed the tendency to be illiterate in several languages. K. Fagan, in a letter to the same paper, wrote of having his attention drawn by 'Dublin Bus's relatively new Airlink buses (nos. 747, 748 etc.). I was admiring the way Dublin Bus had the destinations painted in French, Italian and German, until I read the latter: "Bus Verbindung Zu den Bus und ZAGBAHNOFEN in Dublin". This translates as "Bus connection to the bus and timid (flinching or faint-hearted) station oven in Dublin"'[35] In which, perhaps, to cook a GOOSE PIE, as the Parliament on College Green, now the Bank of Ireland, was known in its political heyday, on account both of the shape of its premises and the perceived quality of its rhetoric.

OFF CENTRE

The '*commodius vicus* of recirculation' that took Joyce, in *Finnegan's Wake*, 'from swerve of shore to bend of bay' would need, now, substantially to enlarge its circumambience, and as the city has expanded so has the glossary of its vernacular vocabulary. Suburbs, particularly those seen in need of a little spin to render them more marketable, have rediscovered themselves as 'villages', while real villages beyond the Pale are now an endangered species. The staid suburb/village of Stillorgan, however, is unlikely to rejoice in its reincarnation as MICKEY MARBH (< mickey, penis + Ir. *marbh*, dead). Thus Ross O'Carroll Kelly: 'I have to seriously lead-foot it up to Stillorgan – mickey marbh, as they say in the west'.[36] Sallynoggin, technically in the new county of Dún Laoghaire/Rathdown, has given birth to the common noun SALLY (head), losing its noggin in the process. Further south again, Carrickmines briefly rejoiced in the presence of the CARRICKMINDERS, protesting against the destruction of a medieval castle to make way for a motorway. 'Even their initial tactics,' complained Liam Reid, 'echoed those of the Wood Quay protesters more than a quarter of a century earlier.'[37] Further along the same motorway, the M50, its intersection with the N7 and the LUAS was to become a byword for endemic circulation problems. 'He had an idea how to encounter the most vicious insect in Pandora's Box,' the *Irish Independent* wrote of the then Minister for Transport, Séamus Brennan: 'to prevent tailbacks, and possibly terrible accidents where the rail line will cross the M50 at the Red Cow Roundabout [< the Red Cow, an adjacent hostelry] – THE MAD COW ROUNDABOUT, as it will forever be known.'[38] (The Minister's brainwave, to put the LUAS on stilts, never got off the ground.)

GREENHOUSE EFFECT

On the northside, a bit beyond the NALL or NALLER (Royal Canal) and the NORRIER (North Circular Road), the now toppled or top-pling towers of high-rise Ballymun are simply BALLYER. Drumcondra, or DEDRA, is a near neighbour to Glasnevin's Botanic Gardens, known to all Dubliners, north and south, as THE BOTS, renowned for their Victorian greenhouses. (In the city centre, however, GREENHOUSES were street urinals, so named from the colour they were painted). And in the same neighbourhood, southside prejudices could not but have been reinforced by Séamus de Burca's invitation 'Ah musha, if you want the FUNK (smell) of pigsties take a walk along Phibsborough Road!'[39] Drumcondra also embraces Croke Park, the headquarters of the GAA, or GAH, equally universalised as CROKER. 'Before it was Croke Park' according to Fiona Looney, 'it was the City and Suburban Racecourse, known locally as Jones's Road'.[40] Its homophone, CROAK PARK, is applied to Glasnevin cemetery, former resort of bodysnatchers, or SACK-EM-UP MEN. The DRUMCONDRA MEDALLISTS, according to the theatrical historian Christopher FitzSimon,[41] were a group of local residents who habitually entered for com-petitions in the minor arts of verse-speaking, ballad-singing and step dancing. The Bon Secours Hospital, run by nuns and thus colloquially THE BUNCH OF HOORS, is built on the site of Dalville, the mansion of Swift's friend Dr Delaney and his voluble wife, while one of the most reviled northside locations is the markedly unhi-larious penitentiary known as THE JOY, aka Mountjoy Jail, with its characteristic gong immortalised by Brendan Behan as THE AULD TRIANGLE which 'goes jingle-jangle along the banks of the Royal Canal'. The same canal used to boast a branch which led to Broadstone over Foster Aqueduct, popularly the ACHE-A-DOC, demolished in 1951.

JANEY MACK

Towards the end of the eighteenth century, the undeveloped dis-trict lying between the canal and the River Tolka was known as

MUD ISLAND, famous in the 1600s for 'the daring deeds of its denziens'[42] who were, in fact, a motley collection of thieves, highwaymen and smugglers who boasted their own 'king'. In this vicinity, at a later date, was located the equally notorious Mecklenburg Street. 'Dublin sadly misses its Red Lamp quarter,' lamented Ellis, a character in James Plunkett's novel, *Farewell Companions* (1977): 'It used to be concentrated around Mecklenburg Street but the clergy and the Legion of Mary succeeded in killing it off when the British left. Have you heard about it? It was known as MACK TOWN in Gogarty's time.'[43] The name came from the formidable Mrs Mack, one of the best-known of the brothel madams. (If whores are most generally women, HOORS, on the contrary, are invariably of the male sex.) The area which Joyce dubbed NIGHTTOWN took in Montgomery Street, named for Elizabeth Montgomery who became the wife of the eighteenth-century property developer Luke Gardiner, subsequently Lord Mountjoy. It was also known as THE DIGS, THE KIPS or MONTO – though Bella Cohen's brothel, or FLASH HOUSE, the focus of the 'Circe' episode in Joyce's *Ulysses*, was located in Upper Tyrone Street. Corporation Street, which traversed the brothel area, has been renamed James Joyce Street in honour of one of the most consistent patrons of the UNFORTUNATE GIRLS or just UNFORTUNATES: 'And there were some prostitutes on the docks … Now we had two – I always used to call them "two ladies"… they were unfortunates – and they used to have a stand at the back of the Gas Company.'[44]

If the street names, and the nicknames, are now nothing but a faded memory of the oldest profession (LUGS Brannigan, a Garda with a style all his own, consistently referred to its members as PAVEMENT HOSTESSES), it was not entirely banished from the area: Doran's pub, in Marlborough Street, established in 1889, where you could buy lunchtime oysters from an itinerant salesman as late as the late 1950s, was one of the first of Dublin's modern lounges, where women were able to go alone for a drink. 'Dublin wags, ever-inventive and in reference to the closeness of the city's Catholic cathedral, used to call it THE PRO'S CATHEDRAL.'[45] At the other extreme, so to speak, Trinity Hall, Dartry, the closely guarded southside residence for female Trinity students (or JIBLETS, < JIB, a first-year male undergraduate) after some 64 years finally opened its doors to the predatory sex. In 1972, the College paper, *Trinity News*, announced 'VIRGINITY HALL is no more ...'

FRINGE EVENT

Both Drumcondra and Ringsend lay within the old city limits, known as FRINGES, a corruption of 'franchises'. Thus John Edward Walsh:

> To guard themselves from encroachment, the citizens from time immemorial perambulated the boundaries of their char-
> tered district every third year, and this was termed 'riding the franchises', corrupted into RIDING THE FRINGES.[46]

The practice was inaugurated in 1192 and continued, if in a restricted form, until the close of the eighteenth century. Some of the colloquial names to be found within these boundaries, in particular in what is now the city centre, are in many instances of almost equal antiquity. The houses built in the Coombe in or around 1670, with their gables facing onto the street, were known as DUTCH BILLIES after the Prince of Orange, the future King William III. The passageway leading down from Christ Church Place to the quays was formerly known as HELL:

> The old passage-way got its name from a carved emblem of the Devil that stood over the arched entrance ... Its fame extended beyond the shores of Ireland, being mentioned by the poet Burns in one of his poems.[47]

Hell was, less dramatically, the workplace of a master-cutler who gave his name, SINGLETON, to a highly efficient corkscrew. The area was also reputed to be haunted by one Olocher, a convicted murderer, whose ghost took the form of a huge black pig. According to Patrick F. Byrne, 'a woman swore before magistrates that she had seen THE DOLOCHER, for by now this is what the Dublin people christened the apparition.'[48] The Dolocher, however, turned out to be a man dressed in a black pig's skin.

CHANGING LANES

Many of Dublin's older thoroughfares reflect the occupations of their original inhabitants: thus Cook Street was formerly THE STREET OF THE COOKS. It is difficult in some cases to distinguish between names and nicknames, but the fact that not a few of them were sanitised in staid Victorian times suggests the latter, even if the derivations proved otherwise. According to T. Dawson:

> In 1876, the Nationalist members of the Corporation, thinking it might be a good thing to keep Cromwell's deeds before us, changed CUT-THROAT LANE to Roundhead Lane and MURDERING LANE to Cromwell's Quarters. 'Cut-throat' was a corruption of the name Coitrot, a family who lived there at one time, and Cromwell's Quarters are more popularly known in the neighbourhood as the FORTY STEPS which lead to Bow Lane and Bow Bridge ...[49]

Another passageway, leading from Dame Street to Dame Court, hard by what used to be Hely's Acme Printing Works, was known as Acme Arch until the propensity of some citizens to refer to it as ASK ME ARSE hastened a change of name. ('Now don't be givin me any a dat YIS were very lucky against Kildayer shite ... Brootle. Dee only way ta describe dem. Jason Sherlock? ASK ME BLEEDIN ARSE.[50]) Another narrow and in this case steeply graded thoroughfare,

Keyzar's Lane, leading to Cook Street, was known, in the same vein and no doubt on account of its propensity to induce a loss of equilibrium, as KISS ARSE LANE. Some minor thoroughfares were renamed more than once. According to T. Dawson, 'Picot's Lane became in turn Lovestoke's Lane, Longstick Lane, Woodstock Lane, before being named Rosemary Lane, its final one'.[51] In 1753, the Corporation found it necessary to increase the water supply to the expanding city. To achieve this, they 'tapped the Grand Canal at its highest point', according to Brian Mac Giolla Phádraig,[52] 'and had the water conveyed in elmwood pipes to the City Basin in St James' Street. THE BACK OF THE PIPES, a passageway from Dolphin's Barn to the Basin, is still remembered'. The pipes ran along an elevated rampart known as THE RIDGES.

HOLDING YOUR CORNER

As befitted a small and intimate city, many locations retained the names of individuals in popular parlance long after they had departed the scene. Seamus Martin wrote of a shop as the junction of Upper Camden Street and Harcourt Road:

> The more investigative observer can see in the building's recessed doorways the name Kelly inscribed in the same type [as the legends 'cigar bonder' and 'tobacco blender']. For this is the Kelly's shop that gave the name KELLY'S CORNER to the entire crossroads ... Bus tickets on certain routes bear the imprint 'Kelly's Corner' in blue ink.[53]

Alderman James Kelly, in addition to being a tobacconist, was High Sheriff of the City of Dublin in the early twentieth century. From Kelly's Corner, Camden Street leads down to Aungier Street, which, wrote James Plunkett in *Farewell Companions*, 'had seen so many ambushes [during the War of Independence] that it was known popularly by now as the DARDANELLES'.[54] For

45

some reason, corners, the preferred location of the city's virtually immobile CORNER BOYS of yesteryear – loiterers without intent – continued to enshrine individual identities in the popular memory. Thus J.L.J. Hughes, writing of 'Dublin Street Names': 'The present Doyle's Corner at Phibsborough I knew as DUNPHY'S CORNER. If a person was asked to explain a morning's absence from work he might reply that he had GONE ROUND DUNPHY'S CORNER, meaning that he had attended a funeral to Glasnevin Cemetery.'[55] 'It was accepted that this was where you would end your days,' wrote C.S. Andrews: 'passing the LONG CORNER as Doyle's Corner ... was generally known then.'[56]

Going around St Mary's Chapel of Ease, popularly the BLACK CHURCH, was somewhat more hazardous. 'As children,' wrote Austin Clarke, 'we were told that anyone who ran round the church three times after dark would meet the Devil on the third time round.'[57] The result of such an inauspicious meeting might have consigned the victim to the CATACOMBS, which, however, was a repository not so much of old bones as of those perennially OSSIFIED in the colloquial Dublin sense of the word. A resort of impecunious writers and their hangers-on in the 1950s, the Catacombs, recalled Anthony Cronin, 'had once been the basement, composed of kitchen, pantries and wine-cellar ... of one of those high Georgian mansions [in Fitzwilliam Street] that are the pride of Dublin ... Most of what went on in the Catacombs was in fact ordinary social boozing. Where there is booze, it will usually prevail over other matters.'[58]

If Hell, the Black Church and the Catacombs were no more than intimations of mortality, local names often reflected closer encounters. The Templeogue Inn was known as THE MORGUE on account of the succession of inquests held there on people who fell victim to the Dublin and Blessington Steam Tramway which passed the door. On the other side of the city, wrote Edgar F. Keatinge, 'Many men were killed on the Lucan Road [coming from the markets asleep on their carts] and that their bodies were brought to the pub where the inquest was held, and so it became known as THE DEAD MAN'S PUB [or more usually just THE DEAD MAN'S].'[59] The arrival of the Dublin & Lucan Steam Tramway (June 1881) was instrumental in perpetuating the name.

HEY NODDY

The introduction of public transport to the city was to generate a distinctive local vocabulary from the era of the sedan chair onwards. With the development of horse-drawn transportation, the available services greatly expanded, and with them the attendant vocabulary. The early conveyances included one-horse vehicles peculiar to Dublin, among them the RINGSEND CAR, so named because it plied principally to that place, then a popular sea-bathing resort. As a mode of transport it left a lot to be desired, as is apparent from a reference by Theophilus Cibber in a letter of 1753: 'There he straddles over the buttocks of the horse with his pedestals on the shafts, like the driver of a Ringsend Car furiously driving through thick and thin, bedaubed, besplashed, besmattered and besmeared.'[60] The NODDY, capable of conveying two people, derived its name from its characteristic backwards and forwards oscillation when in motion. Its driver was known as the NODDY-BOY. In that it ran on four wheels, the JINGLE was somewhat more user-friendly, though its construction habitually produced the jangling that gave it its popular name. There was also a curious conveyance known as the CHAISE-MARINE or chair-marine, a one-horsed low cart with a barred 'float' on the back ends of the shafts. Though originally used for merchandise and goods, it could be adapted for human conveyance by the addition of mats. A letter from a Dublin gentleman to a friend in England, written in 1764, described it as 'the drollest, merriest curricle you ever saw' (a curricle was a light, two-wheeled carriage) and recounted meeting many of these 'featherbed parties' (for 'the gentler sort of people', he explained, the mats were replaced by a bed) coming out of Dublin as he travelled towards the city after landing at the then Dunlary (now Dún Laoghaire).[61] In 1819, an English family of father and daughter visited Joseph Hutton, of the family of the prominent Dublin coachbuilder John Hutton.

> From this visit we returned in an outside JAUNTING CAR, the most pleasant conveyance to those who have not been accustomed to them ... These carriages have been very common here in the streets of Dublin but seem to be giving way to another kind which are called INSIDE CARS and are much more comfortable carriages ...[62]

HORSING AROUND

The habit of affluent Dublin gentlemen of maintaining their own coaches persisted well into the nineteenth century, and it was the thing to be known to be proficient in HANDLING THE RIBBONS. In 1826, Farrell and Sons, coachmakers of Dorset and Dominic Streets, advertised for sale a wide range of vehicles including 'one new Landau, one new Chariot ... two CHARABONGS ... several STANHOPES, DENNETS and TILBURYS'.[63] Among the many who, however, were obliged to make use of public transport, including outside cars or OUTSIDERS, were habitual fare-dodgers, and SCONCING the cabman, or DOING A RUNNER, was a popular pastime. 'A favourite jumping-off spot', according to Frank Hopkins, 'was the Four Courts, where they could make their escape through any one of a large number of doors.'[64] Cabs, forerunners of the taxi or JOE MAXI, were to be engaged at a HAZARD, or cab-stand, a term apparently, if obscurely, from old French, *hazard*, meaning chance: 'Mr Bloom went round the corner and passed the droop-ing nags of the hazard'.[65] 'The hackney drivers and cabbies stand-ing with whips held aloft, advertising themselves with CAR YER HONOUR or CAB-ME-LADY, were more often city individuals and were equally noted for their witticisms ...'[66] This mode of transport also gave rise to local locutions such as 'she has a face like the back of a cab'.

Horse buses were introduced to the city in 1848 and horse trams some 30 years later, bringing with them their own colourful terminology. Collisions with other horse-drawn vehicles were not uncommon, a product of arrogance on the part of the tramway men and carelessness or aggression on the part of other drivers. According to Michael Corcoran,[67] 'Those in charge of other horse-drawn vehicles were often guilty of speeding ... such individuals were widely referred to as JEHUS, a title derived from the Book of Kings.' (They were most usually owner-drivers, whereas the driver of the Dublin taxi of the future would often be a COSIE, or co-driver, sub-contracting the vehicle from the owner for twelve hours out of the 24). C.S. Andrews recalled excursions to the Strawberry Beds, then a noted beauty spot, 'organised by some benevolent society and they set off in DRAGS, a kind of long car drawn by two horses and seating about twelve people sitting face to face'.[68] Funerals generally demanded the service of four horses. The pair harnessed immediately in front of the hearse did most of the work and were referred to as WHEELERS. 'The drivers had semi-tall hats and the cortege proceeded through the streets at walking pace. Widows wore WIDOW'S WEEDS, a large black, thick veil which covered the head to the shoulders'.[69]

BRAKING POINT

'The Dublin streets that I first knew thudded and neighed and whinnied with every kind of horse that can be imagined,' wrote the poet and novelist, James Stephens, born in 1882. 'And they also snorted and screamed with kinds of horses that can't now be imagined at all. For example, there was a horse then which you cannot now meet anywhere: he was broodingly, perhaps proudly, referred to as a WICKED HORSE ...'[70] Amongst this class of animal were those on delivery duties — milk, coal and virtually every other domestic requirement — which, once having got the bit between their teeth, were disinclined to stop. Calls to horses are amongst the oldest forms of verbal communication anywhere. 'It was hair-raising to watch the driver bent backwards like a rodeo rider straining and pulling on the reins, yelling HIKE, HO-THERE, HO THERE'.[71] The thousands of such horses used for commercial transport by business big and small up to the Emergency (and given a new lease of life then by the shortage of petrol) were broken in by a NAGSMAN to get them used to city traffic. 'The slang word for horse dealers in them days was RAZOR BLADES, 'cause they used to cut one another's throat in the opposition. And at a horse fair another fella he'd be trying to SHARP you — a slang word — trying to GET INSIDE YOU.'[72]

HORSE POWER

The horse-trams themselves had offered something short of rapid transit. As Edgar F. Keating observed: 'in those days there was much more of a hill leading up to Portobello Bridge, and it was a fascinating sight to me to watch the HITCH-BOYS as they stood waiting with an extra hitch-horse, or COCK horse, ready to hitch to the next tram and help the other two horses to pull their load up the hill'.[73]

'Away in a tram from Nelson's Pillar they went for miles and miles', wrote Sean O'Casey: 'having first managed Cork Hill where the two tram horses were helped by another, called a PULLEY-UP ...'[74] Hitch-horses also assisted at Newcomen Bridge on the northside, where they were known as TIP-HORSES, originally meaning horses that pulled wagons to a tip-head. Conductors were exhorted to take firm action against SCUTTING (see below) and were warned against TREATING — allowing passengers to travel without paying a fare. (A young lad caught scutting might well be described as a SCUT. Thus Killian Doyle: 'I remember seeing TV footage of Red China when I was a mere scut of a boy'[75]). 'Drivers were required to be agile as well as responsible, according to Sean O'Casey: 'The driver LEPPED down off his platform, unhooked the TRACING-POLE with one hand, turned the horses to the opposite end of the tram by the reins with the other, hooked the tracing-pole again, and climbed onto the platform'.[76] (It should be noted that there is a world of difference between a LEPPER and a BUCKLEPPER, a term said to have been invented by the poet Patrick Kavanagh to denote an ignorant mode of ostentatious behaviour which passed into the vernacular. As for lepper itself:

What's a lepper?
    It's unfortunate people with a terrible disease that makes their limbs fall off.
How can they LEP if they're like that?
    They don't lep. They walk around slowly.
What are they called 'leppers' then?
    Would you not BE ASKING idiotic questions. [77])

A contributor to the website overheardindublin.com reported that shortly after the introduction of the smoking ban in 2004:

I was standing outside a pub having a smoke when I overheard two OUL' ONES in conversation. One said 'JAYSUS this smoking ban is a pain in the arse'. To which the other replied 'I know, jaysus ... we're like bleedin' LEOPARDS out here'[78]

Another variation on the animal theme comes from the same source:

Old lady: Jaysus, I'm like her bleedin' maid doin' everything for her.
Friend: She sounds like she's treating ya like an ESCAPED GOAT ...[79]

MIND THE TRAMS!

The electric trams, at their peak in the 1920s and 1930s and constituting one of the finest urban systems in Europe, were the repository of much familiar terminology. WAYLEAVE, for instance was 'a form of toll paid by the DUTC.[Dublin United Tramway Co.] to the Dublin Corporation for the privilege of laying down tram-lines in public thoroughfares'[80] 'There are still some Dublin residents who talk of THE TRAM STABLES,' wrote Raymond O'Donoghue in 1984.[81] On the eve of the 1916 Rising, C.S. Andrews was in Terenure: 'When I arrived at the tram stop ... I noticed something unusual. The trams had halted and some of them were pulling into the stables.'[82] The early tram, known as the RATTLER (for a later, less innocent, generation, to RATTLE was to indulge in sexual intercourse), departed the city centre at 05.35 and was, according to an anonymous writer in *The Irish Times* in the early years of the Emergency, 'almost a private car, reserved for the select few ... the majority of the passengers are bakers, bound for factories at Ballsbridge and Dun Laoghaire.'[83] Earlier than that, in the small hours, a distinctive maintenance vehicle, the GHOST TRAM, had slid silently along the complex network of tracks. (Large dental braces were then known as TRAM TRACKS.) Paddy Crosbie recalled the DIRT TRAM which 'used come up from the quays along Queen Street, and through George's Lane on its way to Stanley Street'[84] – the location of the CORPO's refuse destructor plant. The CROSS TRAM was the number 18, the one service which avoided the city centre. The Dollymount line was subject to serious flooding, and a special high-clearance tram for use in these emergency periods was introduced in 1926, referred to as the STORM CAR or colloquially the SUBMARINE. The playwright Denis Johnston recalled this conveyance, No. 80, 'with the green shield for Dollymount borne on two spikes above the destination indicators', as well as a Terenure tram, No. 191, 'affectionately known as THE COFFIN from its hexagonal ends'.[85] Early-morning cars on some routes, particularly on Saturdays and Mondays, were known as

PAWN TRAMS from the number of women heading for the pawn-broker's, or PEOPLE'S BANK. Brendan Behan's mother could have been among them: 'By the time I RELEASE Da's suit and a couple of other things there'll be little left of either of their wages.'[86]

SHEETS IN THE WIND

The elegant balcony cars which operated on the Dalkey line were known as WINDJAMMERS. 'A feature of these trams', according to Michael Corcoran, 'was a canvas sheet on each platform which could be unrolled and fastened to close off the stairwell, thus protecting the motorman from the elements. The similarity to a flapping sail probably inspired the nickname.'[87] When these trams were full, they were known as SWINGERS, from their tendency to sway. The actor Eamon Morrissey recalled:

> There was a Dublin expression used in our family when you were moving something heavy and wanted everyone to lift together. You said: NOW, DALKEY. It was apparently based on an OULD SNOT of an inspector in O'Connell Street who would stand eyeing his watch, and when the appointed time for departure came, would slap the side of the tram with his fist and roar: 'Now, Dalkey.'[88]

Inside the vehicle, the conductor punched the multicoloured tickets in his CLICKETTY. Moira Lysaght remembered:

> Many of the conductors were noted for their running comments as they called out stopping points, adding their own explanatory definitions such as 'St........'s Road, LODGER'S ALLEY.'[89]

ON THE BUTTON

Additional passenger capacity was provided by a seat at the top of the car called the BUTTON, also known as the PIANO-STOOL. 'This was a movable round-topped seat', Paddy Crosbie remembered, 'which screwed into the floor in front of the sliding doors at each end of the tram ... My father explained that it was placed in front of one of the doors to prevent passengers leaving the tram by the wrong exit, once the tram had stopped at a terminus.'[90] Trams had poor headlights and no windscreen wipers, making driving at night a hazard. There were various techniques employed to improve the driver's vision: '... some people used to slice a potato in two and rub the window with the potato ... Did you ever hear of GOBOIL? Well, we'd do that (put some spit or saliva) on the glass.'[91] Conditions for the drivers on the Howth Hill service, axed in 1959, were equally demanding, as Tom Redmond, the last of them, remembered: 'You got no meal break at any time. Drivers' wives would have to bring you a few sandwiches and what we called a TOMMIE CAN of tea, a small can that'd hold about a pint.'[92] 'Tram' was also employed as a verb, as, for example, 'Mr Bloom passed on out of the clanking noises through the gallery on to the landing. Now am I going to TRAM it out all the way and then catch him out perhaps?'[93]

ON THE BUSES

Dublin city's fine tramway system finally succumbed to the blight of the motor bus in 1949, with the closure of the Dalkey line ('the trams are all GONE FOR THEIR TEA', as Éamonn MacThomáis lamented[94]). Buses had begun to appear in numbers after the Great War, independent companies competing recklessly and frequently unscrupulously with one another to pick up fares. 'Names such as the BLUE LINE, the CARMEL, the PIRATE and the FALCON were well known to city travellers of the '30s.'[95] Though in those traffic-free times faster and more manoeuvrable, somehow buses failed to attract the grudging affection bestowed by the travelling public upon the trams. Occasional changes in livery might produce popular allusions — witness the brief era of the stunningly yellow single-decker BANANA BUSES, and, much later, the BENDY BUSES. In Tallaght, though, the former name was to carry a different reference. According to local resident Bob Byrne, '... we now have eighteen routes in and out of the city centre, but the schedule is ridiculously planned. Nothing for ages then a crop of them all together. We call them banana buses because they come in bunches.'[96] But in general the buses lacked character and individuality; perhaps only the GARAGE BUS, the homing saviour of the (relatively) late-night reveller before the era of Nitelink, found a firm place in the lexicon, together with the unfortunate 46A, which for some reason became a joke and a symbol for the traditional vehicle which, after an unconscionable waiting time, arrives in threes. Though strictly a one-passenger conveyance, the POPEMOBILE was a Dublin-named and created bullet-proof vehicle first employed in the Phoenix Park on 29 September 1979 on the occasion of the visit of Pope John Paul II.

LUAS TALK

With the introduction of free travel for over-65s, Dublin buses became the target of TWIRLIES (< am I too early?), 'innocently' attempting to avoid paying the fare demanded of all during the city's morning and evening peak periods. Trams were to reappear in minimal form some half-century later in the shape of the unlinked two-line Luas (< Irish *luas,* speed) which almost immediately found itself a couple of nicknames. 'On arrival at St Stephen's Green,' enthused Fergus Cassidy of the inaugural trip on the Green Line, 'nostalgia gave way to delight at the speed, comfort and style of the journey. The JERRY LEE is here to stay — and hopefully the slang along with it.'[97] Those with a somewhat different cultural orientation, however, opted for the histrionic, or even, claiming topographical superiority, the poetic: '... the goy's heading straight towards him like a focking DANIEL DAY about to plough into a cor on, like, Middle Abbey Street.'[98] 'The DANNY DAY', commented Mr Day-Lewis himself: 'Wasn't it a toss-up between that and Jerry Lee? It's a relief to have a tram named after you rather than a public toilet.'[99] To northsiders Luas may be the DANIEL DAY or the JERRY LEE, wrote Séamas Ó Maitiú from rural County Chill Mhantáin, 'but to southsiders like myself it is, of course, the CECIL DAY or the C.S.'[100] According to Anne Marie Hourihane, the driver of the first Luas, Eddie Byrne, can spot not only the fare dodgers but 'the tram enthusiasts — known as TRAMSEXUALS — who like to tour the world photographing trams'.[101] But for how long will the Luas continue to hold centre-stage? 'Madam', wrote John Devlin, 'I read there is a proposal for a cable car system running above the River Liffey. Will it be known as the SUAS?'[102]

TRAINS OF THOUGHT

Dublin's first railway, which opened between Westland Row and Kingstown (now Dún Laoghaire) in 1834, was popularly the FRIENDS' LINE on account of the high level of Quaker involvement in its financing and construction. The only other railway to impact on the urban area until recent times was the Dublin and South Eastern, running from Harcourt Street to Bray, which became known as the DIRTY, SLOW AND EASY (alternatively and less popularly, DAMN SLOW AND EASY, even just the SLOW AND EASY). According to Eoin O'Brien:

> The Dublin and South Eastern Railway was the link, the placental cord ultimately to be severed, between home and the city of Dublin and the world beyond. Foxrock Station and its train, the 'Slow and Easy', were to leave lasting memories with [Samuel] Beckett ...[103]

According to Brian Mac Aonghusa, its modest city terminal was referred to by the citizens as an egg: 'a lovely shell on the outside with just a yolk [YOKE – any unspecified object] inside'.[104] There was only one platform. The Dublin and Blessington Steam Tramway, a cross between a tram and a train, and remarkable for the number of accidents occurring to unwary or incapacitated pedestrians, became popularly known as THE LONGEST GRAVEYARD IN THE WORLD. During the relatively rare peak periods, this tramway utilised timber bogies fitted with temporary seating and protective wire mesh; these odd vehicles were known, predictably, as CAGE CARS. The leisurely pace sustained by the city's public transport system as a whole was generally regarded as being exemplified in its adopted symbol, a lateral development of the circle and centre line device of the Paris Metro/London Underground, and nicknamed the FLYING SNAIL.

The surviving Dublin suburban line from Howth to Bray was electrified in 1984 and renamed the DART (Dublin Area Rapid Transit), 'a name which has led many a wag to proclaim that: "Isn't it a good thing now that Dublin wasn't called Florence?"'.[105] Initially scorned by the BEGRUDGERS as CIÉ'S GREEN ELEPHANT (< its colour scheme) its impact on the city was to prove not only economic but phonetic (see Chapter 3). Its effect on property values along its route became known as DARTIFICATION, creating the affluent *terrain vague* which became known as DORTLAND. Its motive power is supplied by overhead wires, not seen in the city since the demise of the trams. 'The work over the Christmas period [2003]', wrote Joe Humphries, 'will tackle a particularly troublesome maze of overhead cabling, or CELESTIAL KNITTING as it's known in the business'.[106]

GO N-ÉIRÍ AN ROTHAR LEAT

Back on the streets, other modes of transport also enriched the popular lexicon. 'Where would you be goin' with no bell on your bicycle?' – the conversational gambit attested to the virtual universality of that simple form of conveyance in the pre-car era. 'His bicycle was the tallest he had seen,' wrote Bob Quinn, 'what they called an UPSTAIRS MODEL, a big black-framed machine which he pushed with one hand.'[107] If you were in luck, the owner might have offered you a CROSSER – a ride on the crossbar. (A BICYCLE also connoted, in its derogatory Dublin sense, someone who was bisexual, or 'pedalling with both feet', as well as an available woman or EASY RIDE.)

Paddy Crosbie recalled, 'Although money was AS SCARCE AS HOBBY-HORSE MANURE, my father managed to produce a bicycle for the three of us, Mossy, Mona and myself. We took our turns using the bike, which was a girl's model'[108] A HIGH NELLIE was, as the name implies, a singularly tall ladies' model with a distinctive curved bar on the frame. Kids lacking bicycles practised the art of SCUTTING – jumping onto the back of moving cabs or lorries for a free ride, or GOFFO. Those failing to make the jump would meanly shout SCUT THE WHIP! or SCUT BEHIND! as a warning to the driver that unauthorised persons were aboard, and then run LIKE THE CLAPPERS. Smaller citizens had their own means of transport. According to Rose Doyle, 'Kevin Anderson's first memory, when he was just a few years old in 1918, is of being pushed across Dublin in his wickerwork GO-CAR.'[109] Not specific to any known form of personal transport, the dismissive concession WE HAD ONE BUT THE WHEEL CAME OFF IT was generally effective in putting an UPPITY individual back in his (or her) box.

THANKFUL FOR SMALL MERCS

Later youthful generations graduated from home-made BOX-CARS, or TROLLEYS, also requiring a good push, to the self-propelled real thing, known to old-timers as MOTORING CARS. Later, lethal COMPANY CARS, or old bangers, could be acquired illegally or for a very modest outlay, and raced down the Stillorgan DUALLER (dual carriageway). If pursued by a SPEEDY, or Gárda motor-bike, a driver of such a JAMMER might PULL A HANDBRAKER in an effort to elude capture. 'Some nights', wrote Harry McGee, kids 'will make their way over to new estates in Lucan and steal cars from streets and car parks. They will then make their way back, joyride them – or RALLY them, to use their own phrase, and burn them'.[110] The drivers of such vehicles would be most unlikely to hold a licence, while many, including otherwise law-abiding bikers, get by on a succession of provisional licences. 'Hibernian [Insurance] says 90 per cent of all pillion passenger claims come from those who've come a cropper off the back of some PROVO's bike'[111] – not, of course, to be confused with a member of a long-established illegal organisation.

If such vehicles, and their drivers, fall somewhat short of the ideal, the HALF CAR is in an altogether different category. The name, out of the same stable, so to speak, as the HALF-SIR, applied to the son of a gentleman farmer rather than a 'full' gentleman, denoted the chauffeur-driven means of transport accorded to a junior government minister, a step or two down from the Mercedes awarded to his or her seniors. 'Labour's Tommy Broughan ... said Mr Dempsey should take direct responsibility for the Bill, given that the department's occupier of the "half-car", Minister of State Pat the Cope Gallagher, had apparently disapeared'[112] A feature of the Dublin car scene before the advent of multi-storey car parks was the PARKER, some of whom were 'official', belonging to a union and sporting badges, some of whom were not. '... I was a BLUFFER,' confessed Frankie Farrelly. 'That's unofficial. But I'd have me cap and put a green ribbon on it, to let people see you're a car parker ... Ah, but car parkers stuck together ... Sometimes car parkers get barred from pubs 'cause some are MOUTHY and SHOUTY'.[113] Though often abused for neglect of their self-appointed car-minding duties, they were, for better or worse, one of the last vestiges of the Dublin street CHARACTERS.

OUT OF CHARACTERS?

The expanding, increasingly cosmopolitan city has virtually seen the last of them. However, as Robert Gahan wrote:

> But in the old leisurely Dublin, they were better considered ... the streets were then so quiet that little more than the jingle of a passing jarvey's horse and car competed with the cockleman as he went by shouting 'COCKLE-LARGE-COCK' ... then, too, might be heard the plaintive cry of the little woman who seemed to glide like a ghost, her passing only signalled by her plaintive cry of 'Water Cress, WATER GRASS,' thus giving the right name as well as the best-known one.[114]

A character in Roddy Doyle's *Brownbread* (1989) remembers: 'I always connect Mount Pleasant Avenue with a tall black-shawled woman who walked rapidly along the sidewalk with her basket on her head calling "Ye-oung wather grass! Ye-oung wather grass!"'[115] The street characters 'of little account, just old scamps, fond of a drink and an occasional fight' were generally held in amused affection and given nicknames reflective of their eccentricities. Gahan recalls some of them: a trio known as HAMLET, DUNBAR and UNCLE, street performers; THE GRAND OLD MAN, a soldierly figure; SOODLUM; PADDY SUGARSTICK; THE BOMBAY DESERTER, remarkable for having deserted from the British army when stationed in India and somehow making his way home, and many more. Oliver St John Gogarty wrote affectionately of 'an odd figure MOIDERED by memories':

> He was but slightly touched, for he had wit enough to realise his trouble. So, when his doctor told him that his mental disability was likely to become progressive, but that he would never be violently unbalanced, he remarked: 'Endymion, whom the moon loved: a lunatic ...'. So ENDYMION he became ... Dublin saw him only as a man gone NATURAL, and Dublin has outstanding examples in every generation.[116]

Others nearer to our own time were the BIRD FLANAGAN who acquired his name, it was said, from having attended a fancy-dress ball dressed as a bird and laying an egg; and, known to all and sundry in the middle of the last century, BANG BANG. His death on 12 January 1981 was recorded in the *Irish Independent*:

> One of Dublin's best known and most beloved characters Tommy 'Bang Bang' Dudley has died in a home for the blind. He was an institution in Dublin in his lifetime. He carried a huge jail key with him around the city, mockingly pointing it at strangers and shouting 'Bang Bang'.[117]

Perhaps the last of the street characters to attract wide public notice was THE DICEMAN (Thom McGinty) a frequenter of various guises in Grafton Street in the latter decades of the last century. More recently, as Shane Hegarty put it,

> ... the charities of the land woke up and realised that the way to get money from the public was not through the gentle rattle of a collection box but by employing Australian back-packers to harass people. The 'charity mugger' was born. They are now most commonly known as CHUGGERS. Or sometimes by a word that sort of rhymes with it ... You know you are about to be CHUGGED because the hairs begin to prick up on the back of your wallet.[118]

Their muted Grafton Street cries — according to Hegarty, on the lines of 'Hi there, can I talk to you a minute for blind children?' — have little in common with the traditional models. But the latter are not quite a thing of the past. Joe Humphries was in the Phoenix Park for *The Irish Times* on the occasion of the service of remembrance for Pope John Paul II on 7 April 2005, and wrote '... it was like stepping back in time: "Get the last of the Vatican Flags", barked a woman with a roadside stall of chocolate bars,

Tricolours and rapidly disappearing Pope Memorabilia'.[119] And, around Christmas, the same formulaic utterance can still be heard in Henry Street and environs, though perhaps with the onset of modern sophistication, no longer 'Get the last a the jumpin' monkeys ...'

3

DO YOU TAKE
STILUMANTS?

Once upon a time, in an immense inundation of vanity, I
thought the Dublin Man might be analysed through his language. For example, minimum and chromium become MINIUM
and CHRONYUM. A funeral is a FURENAL. There are many such
words. Recently a Dublin Man (a 'newsboy' of sixty-one) told
me that he had got drunk on 'wine' on a certain Sunday, and
having nothing to do while the pubs were closed in the afternoon, appointed himself a car park attendant outside Croke
Park, where a large match was in progress. 'When the crowd
come out,' he said, 'I seen two priests come out. They come
over to me and wan of them looks at me very hard. *Tell me, my
good man,* says he, *do YOU take* STILUMANTS?'

Myles na gCopaleen, 'The Hair of the Dogma'

Metathesis is the technical term, and it remains an enduring
characteristic of a certain category of Dublin speech. Thus
Anto Byrne's 'Diary of a Dublin Football Fan': 'So it's home wit
me *Sunday* WURDLED, into de JACKS to DROP DE KIDS OFF AT DE POOL,
you know YISSER selves, an read de previews a de match sittin on
de bowl.'[1] That short paragraph also illustrates several other
identifiers of Dublinese: the treatment of 'th' (WIT; DE); the plural

63

pronoun (YISSER); A for 'of' the loss of a final voiced consonant (SITTIN); as well as a couple of Dublin phrases or constructions (IT'S HOME WIT ME; YOU KNOW YOURSELF/YISSER SELVES) and a metaphor (DROP DE KIDS OFF AT DE POOL) — all in a context of some 30-odd words. 'Many Dubliners, especially the elderly,' wrote Paddy Linehan, 'had "bad BRONICHALS" from the city pollution.'[2] CRIPS, especially the original Tayto salt and vinegar variety (TAYTO was to become a common noun) were and are a staple of the city diet — the same word in the same sense exists, according to *The Coxford Singlish Dictionary* (2002) in the colloquial English of Singapore.

'In Ireland,' according to Gerald P. Delahunty, 'there are only a small number of distinct accents that are generally and consistently recognised by the adult population, even though many people will be able to make much finer judgements, such as people who can distinguish between five or even six Dublin varieties.'[3] Since that was written, some of these six — if, indeed, that was a fair estimation — have undergone modification, others have virtually disappeared, whilst at least one new type has taken the stage. The foregoing is representative of a typical and apparently enduring Dublin accent, but there is evidence that metathesis is playing a lesser role in the vernacular of today. Certain words, MODREN, for example, and NORTHREN, SOUTHREN, EASTREN are habitually metathesised, even by educated speakers, as in this facetious example from 'De Diary of a Nortside Taoiseach'[4]: 'De Pope helped bring down de Berlin Wall, of course, and I finished de job by welcomin de downtrodden peoples of EASTRIN Europe in de EU.'

OR AND OR

With the growth of the city and the development of communications, very localised accents have come under increasing threat. The Camden Street area is an example. 'There were always large numbers of immigrant people living around here,' Dr Colm Brady told Rose Doyle[5]: 'The early twentieth-century Jewish people have been replaced by Muslim and Hindu groups ... And there was a beautiful, soft Dublin accent that was typical of this area.' Well before that, with the departure of the British, the Protestant/ Ascendancy accent, identified in particular with RAWTHMINES and RAWTHGAR, was in decline. Rathmines, formerly a self-governing suburb, was 'regarded by Irish Irelanders as the epicentre of com-placent British snobbery', wrote Patrick Maume.[6] 'RATHMINES JOHNNIES were young white-collar clerks of high social pretensions, conservative politics and doubtful morals ...' 'The Rathmines accent was a stamp of affectation and parodying, it was a common form of amusement', C.S. Andrews remembered of his childhood.[7] 'THE MUTTING IS ROTTING IN BRITTING STREET [the mutton is rotten in Britain Street] was a favourite example'. But times were changing. Samuel Beckett observed:

> Men of the high standing of the Polar Bear [a nickname], men of culture and distinction, occupying positions of responsibility in the City permit themselves, condescend, to bandy invective with the meanest of day-labourers. Gone is the patrician hauteur, gone, it almost seems, with the Garrison.[8]

The Trinity accent, local to what was until the 1960s a predomi-nantly Protestant institution, was a softer version of the strident Anglo-Irish tones. Beckett had it, as had the majority of his southern contemporaries (Northerners, of whom there were then many among the undergraduates, imported their own idiom).

DESE, DAT AND DOSE

I was over in Fagans when I heard de news from de Vatican. We held a minute's silence wit our pints at half-mast, as a mark of respect. Den I spent de rest of de night watchin de coverage. It's sobering to tink dat I was a new TD, still wet behind de ears, when John Paul II came to power. In fact, dose old pictures of him sharing a platform wit Bishop Casey and Fadder Michael Cleary are a bit like de ones of me wit CJH [Charles J. Haughey] and RAMBO [Ray Burke]. How little de Pope and I knew back den![9]

The long-running satire in *The Phoenix* of Taoiseach Bertie Ahern and his perceived Drumcondra accent masks the fact that the treatment of 'th's is by no means confined to that suburb and dates virtually to the beginnings of Hiberno-English. Thus the character Patrick in Richard Head's *Hic et Ubique, or The Humours of Dublin* of 1663: '... 'tis ill kind for dy Faders shild [child] to be making speech wit dy shelf [self] and no-body.'[10] It remains, if not exclusively, a Dublin characteristic. Mr Dedalus, a Corkman, mocks it in *Ulysses*: 'O weeping God, the things I married into. De boys up in de hayloft.'[11] Irish has no consonant equivalent to the English *th*, either voiced or unvoiced, hence the confusion between that sound and initial or terminal /t/ in Hiberno-English, often reproducing itself in print. Godfrey Fitzsimons noticed that 'at the entrance to Dun Laoghaire's spanking new marina a sign reads "BERTHOLDERS and guests only. Bertholders? Perhaps Bert-holders? I wonder which particular Bert you have to hold to get in there?'[12]

Threads and *treads* are often confused, whilst the *Sunday Tribune* headlined: 'Irish passport recipient THRASHES £15m property'[13] — shades of Basil Fawlty chastising his misfortunate motor car. An anonymous Dublin landlord was interviewing a prominent businessman of Nigerian origin: 'He looked to his two cohorts, picked at his teeth with an ivory TOOT-PICK ...'[14] (It honks when it strikes gold?) That there is an element of class/regional snobbery in attitudes to this particular feature of Dublin pronunciation is apparent: 'We were very taken with Friday's interview on *Morning Ireland* with an official from Dublin City Council,' observed the same source: 'on the subject of the controversial sewage treatment plant in Ringsend. In the course of his chat, he announced that the council would be increasing the size of the plant by a TURD. At least we think that's what he said.'[15]

TEE SHOT

'I think it is awful. And don't fob me off with the usual "Oh Gay! Sure it's part of what we are — it's part of our charm. And it's part of the evolving nature of language and pronunciation ..." and all that bilge. It's nothing more than slovenliness of speech'. Gay Byrne was moved to lengthy criticism of what he described as 'the Soft Irish Tee', directing his fire specifically at the radio and television service of the national broadcaster RTÉ.[16] He chose to represent this phonetic phenomenon by the double /s/ — 'a new eighssy kilomessre bypass' — so that it was not entirely clear what quality of consonant was particularly arousing his ire. It would appear likely, however, that it was the characteristic Dublin voiced/unvoiced 'th' that he was referring to, since he conceded:

> I'm sure the Soft Irish Tee must always have been prevalent. But what intrigues me is that I was never aware of it, certainly on the air, until recently ... I happen to believe that RTÉ, as the national broadcaster, has an obligation to uphold and preserve some decent standards of speech, but at present Montrose is sending a message to all our young people that this is the right way to do it.

Gay's indignation struck a chord with Louis Hogan, writing to the same newspaper:

> Once upon a time RTÉ employed a being called head of presentation. One of his or her functions was to monitor the speech standards of the station's presenters and newsreaders and let them know when they didn't get it right. Words should

be delivered 'as if presented on a silver salver' was one of the dictums emanating from the presentation office. It's far from silver salvers the current lot were reared. RTÉ' speech output is riddled with the soft Irish '*t*' ...[17]

This raises a number of questions apart from the exact quality of this apparently invasive consonant: what are the station's preferred speech standards? Dublin English? More general Hiberno-English? What is known as Received Pronunciation (as practised in the upper echelons of southern England)? And why does Mr Hogan permit himself the luxury of a patently Hiberno-English construction (IT'S FAR FROM ... THE CURRENT LOT WERE REARED) in this critical context? 'The national broadcaster should play a leading role in setting and maintaining proper speech standards,' he concludes. More recently the same station would appear to have taken a decision to Americanise all its dates: 'January fourth, May tenth', in place of the first of January, the fourth of May, etc. One wonders why.

PORT OF WHAT WE ORE?

Louis Hogan's indignation, however, is as nothing compared with the ire aroused by the definitive Dublin dialectical development of the present era, the so-called DORT accent. According to Ailbhe Jordan:

> The germs of this accent existed as far back as the late 1970s in people like Bob Geldof and Bono ... in the 1980s a new yuppie era dawned and with it emerged a new and improved strain. This accent attacked specific geographical regions on the southside of Dublin. Donnybrook and Sandymount were by far the worst affected areas; hence it became known as the 'D4' accent.[18]

With the electrification of the suburban rail services in 1984 under the service name DART, the accent was renamed DORT, though as Francis Kaye wrote, it was 'known in some places as "the AA Roadwatch accent" as the first known victim was Lorraine Keane ... who polluted our airwaves with this accent in the mid-'90s. Why does the Templeogue Roundabout become the TAMPLEOOG RYNDABYTE? Why is south-bound traffic SCYTHE-BYNDE? Why does down-town become DYNE-TYNE?'[19] Other features include 'the irrational use of words such as "like" and "so" in sentences as well as making single word statements like "whatever' and "hello"'. Una Gildea believes: 'infected teenagers tend to raise their intonation as if they were asking a question, a phenomenon linguists refer to as the High Rise Terminal (HRT)'.[20] The latter phenomenon has been blamed on the popularity of Australian soaps such as 'Neighbours', but if these soaps are responsible, Australia is only returning what was originally part of an invisible Irish export. James Beattie, writing of Thomas Sheridan's lectures in Edinburgh 'which I heard him deliver about twenty years ago, distinguished ... the English interrogatory accent from the Irish and Scotch, in this manner. His example was "How have you been this great while?" – in pronouncing which, he observed, that towards the end of a sentence an Englishman lets his voice fall, an Irishman raises his, and a Scotchman makes his voice first fall and then rise'.[21]

NARROW BORES

The strong appeal of the Dart accent to young people, argues Bill Richardson, head of the School of Applied Languages at Dublin City University, is that it is a 'prestige accent', originating within a privileged demographic within Dublin society and connoting a privileged lifestyle, though Paul Cannon of the Irish Association of Applied Linguistics argues that Dart-speakers are a pretentious rather than a prestigious group: 'The so-called Dart accent suggests the rather uneducated nouveaux riches, and a boring superficiality of mind.'[22] What would appear to concern most critics, however — apart from the strangulated vowels — is the likelihood of the accent's pervasive effect not only on other Dublin modes of speech, both in terms of pronunciation and vocabulary, but on the country's wider dialectal richness, already under threat of terminal levelling. As Jeffrey Kallen put it:

> There is a lot of dialect levelling going on in Ireland right now. The local dialects have eroded quite a lot. People are aware of other norms, like American norms and Australian norms and things like that. This is where you get new innovations like this [Dart] accent.[23]

THEME AND VARIATIONS

However, there are innovations even within the innovations. The ubiquitous Ross O'Carroll Kelly, who would appear to have his ear to the ground, or the rail, in this matter, identifies a sequence of northside–southside variants: 'it storts off in, like, Howth and Sutton as THE DOORT. As it makes its way trough Killester and Harmonstown it becomes DE DEERT BUD. Once it clears the city centre and hits SANDYMEISH and Sydney Parade it's, like, THE DAART, DARLING. Booterstown, Blackrock and Monkstown it's, like, THE DORT. . .',[24] followed further south by DE FOOKEN DEEERT and, with a liberal helping of Gay Byrne's soft Irish tee, THE DOORSH.

However much this invasive accent may be deplored by the unfortunates beyond the Pale, it serves to indicate that the levelling process is somewhat short of terminal; and we may perhaps take courage from the prospects for Australian English, a close cousin, the dialectal variations of which have always been relatively limited. According to the lexicographer Kel Richards:

There is a common fear that Australian English is being swamped by Americanisms ... it's certainly true that some adolescent Australians look as if they've been dressed by an emergency relief organisation (wearing trousers two sizes too big) and are trying desperately to sound like inner-city black Americans ... Hence there is this fear that something distinctively Australian (the linguistic equivalent of gum leaves, Bondi beach, beer and barbecues) might be lost under a powerful wave of Uncle Sam-speak. But we're not swamped. Aussie English remains resilient, vigorous and lively ... Aussie English is as linguistically rich as ever and verbal invention seems to be a deep feature of Australian culture. Unless that culture is somehow overturned, we will go on creating locutions — all of them 'bright as a box of budgies'.[25]

Whatever about the prospects for the Dart accent, it is unlikely in the immediate future completely to displace what Una Gildea described as 'the traditional "flat" Dublin accent, which is thought to have originated in the Liberties'.[26] Commonly considered as representative of lower socio-economic groups, aka poor people, it has of late been the focus of what is termed 'inverse prestige' — being deliberately employed by those (almost exclusively male) whose normal mode of speech would reflect that of more affluent city areas. It is a diction and usage, however, subject to many subtleties both of gradation and conscious exaggeration. Hands up, for instance, those who have actually heard a waitress ask 'ARE YA GERRIN' A'?' — Dublinese for 'Are you being served?'

THE SUN, MEWEN AND STARS

There are characteristic features, however, common to most social gradations, as in the pervasiveness of adding extra vowels:

Mrs Diggerty	... we had a great orage — I don't believe, Mr Diggerty, you know what an orage is.
O'Dogherty	Indeed you may take your oath I don't, my dear.
Mrs Diggeerty	That is, sir, because you have not been in foreign parts — then I will tell you what an orage is — sir, it is a STORUM.[27]

Also from the eighteenth century, and roughly from the same decade, comes the slang song, 'De Night before Larry was Stretch'd' which is illustrative of many features of Dublin speech, including both the distinctive 'th' and the addition of the extra vowel, as well as, in a wider human context, the stoical attitude of those incurring the ultimate penalty for what in many cases would now be regarded as petty crime. Larry was no exception:

'Id's all over vid me', says he,
'De neck cloth I'm forced to put on;
And by dis time to-morrow you'll see
Your poor Larry quite dead as de mutton,
Bekase why, his courage was good!'

He is addressing 'de boys' who had come to pay their respects on the eve of execution and are about to engage in a game of cards, using Larry's coffin as a table:

De night before Larry was stretch'd,
De boys dey all ped him a visit;
A bit in deir sacks, too dey fetch'd —
Dey sweated der duds till they RIS it. [pawned]
For Larry was ever de lad,
When a boy was condemned to the squeezer,
To pawn all de togs dat he had,
To help his poor friend to a sneezer [drink]
And WAR-M his gob 'fore he died.

In the original, 'war-m' is given two musical notes, an indication of the extra vowel [/u/ inserted between the two consonants]; and though some of the slang expressions derive from 'Newgate cant', that of the London criminal classes, the vocabulary and syntax of these songs[28] are in many respects pure Dublin.

VOWEL PLAY

The insertion of the additional or epenthetic vowel, as in GREVI-OUS, MISCHIEVIOUS, is also known as 'vowel breaking': 'One morning, in 1774, a poor woman in the house of Industry ... became OUT-RAGIOUS, which was a common expression then to denote a mani-acal outburst on the part of an insane person.'[29] The novelist William Makepeace Thackeray, on a visit to Dublin, overheard 'an active aide-de-camp to the [hotel] doorkeeper roaring "Mr Quiglan, Mr Quiglan! ... a covered KYAR for the Lard Mayre.'[30] "'D'ya know the fat GERREL in the sorting office?"' asked a charac-ter in *Tom Corkery's Dublin*.[31] By the same token, WHITENIN' is for eating, not for painting MURIELS on walls. And a four-syllable WESTMINISTER Abbey is not unheard of, even in polite circles.

Of the distinctive Hiberno-English treatment of the verb, P.W. Joyce wrote:

> Our people ... have a leaning towards the strong inflection, and not only use many of the old-fashioned English strong past tenses, but often form strong ones in their own way – we use SLEP and CREP, old English; and we coin others. 'He RUZ his hand to me', 'I COTCH him stealing the turf ...' 'he HOT me on the head with his stick' ... 'Well, Hyland, are the bullocks sold?' 'Sowld and PED for, sir [see *Larry*, above].'[32]

If not all these have survived from Joyce's century, Dublin still has its fair share of them: 'I SEEN thar, whar 'twas GEV out ... on the Sunday papers', says another of Tom Corkery's characters.

And according to the same writer, 'we are a great crowd for knowing who everybody is ... "I KNEWN that fella", we murmur, when he hadn't a TOSSER.'[33] In a multiple example of verbal singularity, Eamonn MacThomáis 'was caught — ATE, BET and THREW UP again by the Ma ...'[34]

COLOURFUL PAST

The Dublin past tense sometimes takes other unconventional forms:

> 'I'm there mindin me own business with me friend when I
> hear a sairtin voice. Wan guess what the voice was?'
> *'Who owned that voice?'*
> 'Who OWNDED the voice? Are you serious? The brother OWNDED
> the voice, stuck inside the SNUG with four SHAWLIES, two ROZZERS,
> and three Free State Army privates, buyin drinks for all and
> sundry ...'[35]

Anto Byrne and his mates 'voted to set up an action group, Law Abidin' Residents Again de Drugs. "We're not vigilantes or NUTTIN, RIGH, just CONCERNDED parents. De baseball bats IS only for self defence"'.[36] And from Brendan Glacken's vernacular retelling of the Greek legend as *Leda an' de Swan:*

> Leda: I have sumpin to tell ye, Ma — I got tooken advan-
>   tage of.
> The Ma: Whah?
> Leda: Down by the river, Ma.
> The Ma: Never mind where. The ting is, who? Who wazza?
> Leda: It wazza swan, Ma![37]

THE WAN THING

Highlighted in the foregoing are instances of the loss of the final consonant and the employment of the singular of the verb 'to be' for the plural, both common in certain levels of Dublinese. Gay Byrne's former catchphrase, DELIRA' AND EXCIRA', epitomises the former, displaying also the common substitution of the medial /r/ for /t/. 'Angina,' said the young doctor to his female patient. 'Enjoyin' a'?' she retorted, 'YIZ must be jokin'!' In the view of Roisín Ingle '*Desperate Housewives*, or DESPERA' OUL ONES as we on the northside of Dublin like to call the latest US TV phenomenon, has an awful lot to answer for'.[38] The usage, if not the pronunciation, was re-echoed in a contemporary (2005) ad for the Dublin firm, Make-up Forever: 'If the housewives are really DESPERATE how do they manage to look so glamorous?' And as for the no-doubt foreign agency which dreamed up for a sugar substitute the name SPLENDA ... Splenda'!

OUL ONES are more commonly OUL' WANS, both in orthography and pronunciation, members of the extended family that includes YOUNG WANS and just simple WANS — a descending order of denigration. Specifically, OUL WAN can refer to the female parent, otherwise the imported 'old dear', half of the 'old pair'. A WAN of unimpressive appearance and/or habits might have the terms MARY HICK or MARY BANGER applied to her (though BANGER on its own denotes a fart, and, in a related if dated sense, an old car (cf Australian 'old bomb'). A WIGGER is a woman of no importance, whereas a THRILL is suspected of being — or indeed known to be — generous with her person, but persons of either sex are susceptible of being THRILLED SKINNY: 'He is thrilled skinny this nine-year-old boy. This morning he has taken the wheel of his father's powerboat and steered it over a glass-calm sea'.[39] A thrill might also be unflatteringly described as a SCRUBBER, a SLAPPER, a TEASY-WHACKER, or, in respect of favours granted or considered available — a GOOD THING or a RIDE. The latter term, amongst several others of the same genre, transcends the sexual boundary. Thus the schoolgirl usage of Roddy Doyle's *Woman Who Walked Into Doors*: 'We called every fella that wasn't ugly a ride ... Even some of our fathers were rides'.[40] FINE THINGS are equally ambidextrous (Roddy Doyle again): 'I wanked a boy in the back of the room ... Martin Kavanagh, one of the few FINE THINGS in the school ...'

MOT JUSTE

Implying affection rather than disparagement is the quintessentially Dublin MOT, invariably preceded by the definite article. Formerly used of a steady girlfriend or wife (in the latter case frequently THE OUL MOT), it has tended to widen its application to YOUNG WANS in general. Quintessential Dub she may be now, but the mot has been traced back to the eighteenth-century London underworld and beyond into a debatable etymological past.[41] As Diarmuid Ó Muirithe assesses the hypotheses:

> Many lexicographers have connected *mot* with *mort*, another old (sixteenth-century or earlier) cant word meaning a criminal's woman ... Julius Manchon, in *Le Slang* (1923) was the first, I believe, to trace both words to middle Dutch slang *mot,* a prostitute ... He said, in his *Dictionary of the Underworld* (1950) that *mot* was by then obsolete everywhere. He should have asked around Dublin.[42]

In C.S. Andrews' youth:

> The Green Lanes [on the Kimmage Road] provided a coarse form of amusement for younger boys — CLODDING THE MOTS — a game which consisted in finding a pair of lovers stretched in embrace (inevitably involving more than one enthusiastic GOOZER, or kiss) and interrupting their passion by throwing sods of grass and earth on top of them.[43]

If MOT is happily current, you are far less likely to hear DONAH (< Span. *doña,* lady). Seán O'Casey had it: '... an hour ago I and my donah celebrated our diamond wedding in the church of the twelve pathrons [patrons] ...'[44]

FORCE OF HABIT

The singular use of the verb *to be*, as instanced above, is only one of the variations found in the Hiberno-English of Dublin:

> '. . .HER NIBS would take a very poor view of women been brought into the digs after lights out. Wouldn't fancy that at all.
>
> *That is the fashion with all landladies.*
>
> Well the brother DOES HAVE Miss Doy-ull in every night since. They DO WORK very late into the night at the bankin questions.[45]

The habitual present (the Irish verb *bíonn* rendered into English as DOES BE) has, however, been popularly identified with uneducated speakers beyond the Pale. For example, Fiona Looney writes: 'Just this week, coming back from the school, I heard one mother advising another to call on her any time, "because I DO BE GOING there every day". My mom spent years ensuring that her children don't be going anywhere.'[46] (Note the replacement for the traditional MAMMY, now apparently considered distressingly unsophisticated.) But in September 2005, the Taoiseach was widely quoted for his reaction to a controversial consumerist television series: 'I do be annoyed about a lot of things. But I'll tell you — Eddie Hobbs [the presenter] does not annoy me.' The *Sunday Tribune* appended its own southsider comment: 'Bertie Ahern returns from the summer break with a fresh dose of grammatical genius.'[47] If the usage has in recent times taken on something of the stage-Irish, particularly in the urban context, it seems likely for some time to survive the attentions of Fiona Looney's maternal speech police.

EPENTHETIC EXPORTS

The epenthetic (additional) consonant, as in SAIRTINTLY, is also a feature of Dublin pronunciation. Florence Evans, secretary of the Juvenile Advisory Committee 'took a great interest in her work and could tell most amusing stories of her encounters with the young juveniles ... with their tales of "grannies with ULSTERS in their stomachs".[48] Myles na gCopaleen was cornered by a DUBALIN man who had had a disconcerting experience on the way to the AZOO at a time when beasts were still being driven from the Cattle Market along the North Circular Road to the docks:

> I thought to meself, the chap said, that it was a right place to see wild ANGIMALS. I put meself on a 10 bus last THURSDA. We got held up on the way and do you know be what?
>
> *I do not.*
>
> Be wild angimals. TOUSANDS and tousands of heifers and bullocks been BET all over the road by ANGISHORES and PULTOGUES of drovers from the country ... You talk about CRULETY to angimals![49]

The occurrence of the initial and medial additional vowel and the duplicated superlative are neatly encapsulated by Gene Kerrigan:

> No one ever escaped: they always EX-CAPED. You never said something was the same: it was the EX-SAME. No one drowned, though someone might have DROWNDED. Things seldom got worse, though they often got WORSER. You would never follow anyone but you might FOLLY them. You didn't swallow your food, you SWALLIED it. There were no ghosts, only GO-STEZ ... A chimney was a CHIMLEY. The zoo was the IZ-OO. When you went to the cinema you saw a FILLUM.[50]

Alan Roberts wrote:

Suddenly, Betty became as excited as a little girl in a sweet shop. 'He sent YA down a pressie BUT!' She held out a clingfilm package.[51]

Australian linguist Graham Seal noted, among other Irish exports, the tendency, in the eastern states especially and particularly among working-class girls and young women, to end sentences with BUT. 'The folk plural YOUSE, a characteristic of Irish speech, is still so frequently heard around the country that it is included in *The Macquarie Dictionary*.[52] 'Other examples of pronunciation include the pronunciation of words like milk and film as MILUK and FILUM ...'

NON-YOU

Ye know YISSER selves — some strange things happen to personal and possessive pronouns, singular and plural, in the Dublin vernacular, YOUS/YOUSE/YOUZE, YIS/YIZ and YISSER/YIZZER usurping the conventional forms. Thus the archetypical Anto Byrne: 'But sure, wouldn't be DE Dubs if FOLLOWIN DEM was easy, would it? INE [I'm] one A YISSER TICK AND TIN fans. True blue.'[53] The singular is frequently pronounced and written YA, but the conventional 'you' is used in the vocative to terminate a sentence, as in this brief discussion of the origin of life, between two of Sean O'Casey's characters:

Fluther: Mollycewels! What about Adam an' Eve?
The Covey: Well, what about them?
Fluther: What about them, you?[54]

The plural usage is also found in compounds such as HIYIS (hello) and HOWYIS (how are you).

ARTISTIC LICENCE

'There's RAISINS for everything, and currants for cake': the /e/ for /a/ is common at some levels of Dublinese. Samuel Beckett has fun with it: 'From now on she can hold her BAKE altogether or damn well get off the platform ...'[55] And from the other side of the tracks, so to speak, Brendan Behan: 'JIM. You're QUARE and sharp this morning and all.'[56] QUARE is a word of many colours: there are QUARE FELLAS, QUARE HAWKS or HARPS, and QUARE ARTISTS. The young Bob Quinn confronts his preoccupied father:

— What's an artist, Da?
— It's somebody who uses his talents to praise his creator . . .
— You draw pictures. Are you an artist?
— I'm just a doodler. Art is a God-given talent. Real artists spend all their time at it.
— So you're not?
— Not what?
— An artist.
His father suspended his concentration to consider the small nuisance interrogating him. He made an effort.
— Maybe I'm a quare artist.
— What's a quare artist?
— Would you not be annoying me with your questions.[57]

The father's difficulty with the definition stems from the fact that the phrase, in its Dublin usage, is almost indefinable, as is the individual known as a QUARE HARP and the existential location known as the QUARE PLACE. QUARE STUFF is the water of life distilled without legal sanction; whilst employed with the conjunction, as QUARE AN', the phrase is roughly translatable as 'very'.

A somewhat more enthusiastic superlative is the frequently employed TREMENJUS! 'May I put in a plea for tolerating TREMENJOUS as a pronunciation of "tremendous"', inquired D.C. Rose, writing from the Oscar Wilde Summer School: 'in England, this pronunciation is (or was until recently) known as "Old U", or old fashioned upper-class speech "Hijjus" (hideous), "tejus" (tedious), "mejum" (medium) and "Inja" (India) are other examples, as well as our own EEJIT (idiot) ...'[58]

WE NEVER HAD IT THAT GOOD

'Dublin can be heaven with coffee at eleven and a stroll in Stephen's Green ...' — strolling through litter and pools of vomit, averting the eyes from a transmogrified Bewley's café, the closure of which, suggested Nessa O'Mahony, 'was like locking the door of the city's favourite front room, another reminder that the RARE OULD TIMES were DEAD AS DOORNAILS'.[59] (The British colloquial phrase is 'dead as a doornail'. There is no ready explanation as to why the Irish prefer their large-headed nails in multiples, but the simile has been around in one form or another since the four-teenth century). But as with the rare oul' times,[60] forever away and somewhere else, many of the characteristics of Dublinese are in a constant process of change and renewal. Increased mobility, the equivocal benefits bestowed by the Celtic Tiger, the levelling of classes and the consequent virtual extinction of what James Plunkett described as LAWDEDAW combine with the pervasive youth culture and its embracing of media imports to render out of date not a few of the usages and images that have marked the speech of Dublin for much of the modern period. Times have indeed changed since, in the 1960s, the unfortunate Patrick Begley was removed from his job as an RTÉ announcer because he was thought to possess an 'English' accent; it was, in fact, one of the almost-vanished examples of old Dublin upper-class accent, not exclusively Protestant or Ascendancy.

There remain, however, such traces of the past, a persistence of memory, habits of speech governed by ingrained habits of thought and culture, expressed in a distinctive accent that, love it or hate it, shows no real signs of going away. Una Gildea suggested:

> Despite 'working class' areas like East Wall, Rialto and
> Drimnagh being targeted by wealthy first-time buyers in
> recent years, there remains a tendency to look down on areas
> where people speak with flat Dublin accents ...[61]

She goes on to quote two contrary views: 'If somebody spoke with a flat Dublin accent, I'd certainly try to train them out of it, because I don't think it's going to stand to anybody' (Lorraine Barry, proprietor of the Billy Barry stage school). 'I think the Dublin accent is a beautiful accent ... we're one of the few cities in the world that teaches people to be ashamed of the way we speak' (Paul Howard, journalist).

Australian Kel Richards complained:

> I'm often told that I speak for a dying generation, and that the
> next crop of Australian kids will speak only a bland (and
> largely Americanised) form of global English. The evidence is
> otherwise ... Aussie kids are as likely to say 'grouse' as 'cool' or
> 'awesome'. They still know what 'gravel rash' is, while the
> phrase would baffle most Americans ... Aussie kids are display-
> ing the same verbal inventiveness their grandparents did —
> and the source material they're using is the conversation of
> the adults around them, as well as selected bits of imported
> jargon picked up from the media.[62]

There is no reason to suppose that the future development of Dublinese will not follow a similarly vigorous and individualistic pattern.

4

OH! MY! GOD!

Ma: But you HAVE to go to school!

Child (aged 4): I'm not going! I know a-fucking-nuff!

Overheard on the Ballymun bus
www.overheardindublin.com, 20 April 2005

The choice was probably that of the sub-editor rather than the author, but the heading carried by Kevin Williams' article in the 'Rite and Reason'[1] series, 'References to God are part of our language and culture', invoked an ambiguity which was certainly far from what he intended. In the year 1807, William Thomson (real name F.J. Hall, an enquiring Scottish cleric) observed that:

> many of the low people in Dublin are abandoned in the extreme; I heard some women in the streets swearing by the living Jesus, by the Holy Paul, by the blood of the Holy Ghost and the like. One of them, after cursing another, and praying that the devil might hunt her soul, all of a sudden added, 'Arrah, come honey, though you were at Kilkenny and I at Dublin, by the holy cross I would speak well of you.'[2]

Kevin Williams' prime concern was with 'the ghostly rhythm of the [Irish] language that gives expression to a religious worldview' and its perpetuation in the language that replaced it to the extent that 'the prevalence of religious idiom does suggest the enduring place of religious commitment in the hearts and minds of the people of Ireland'. It was no part of his argument to observe how that idiom has been, over the course of the development of Hiberno-English, subverted to more profane ends. The phenomenon is not, of course, confined to English usage or the Irish version of it. In colloquial French, for example, *Jésus* or *petit Jésus* is, or was, used of a male prostitute; Spanish has *¡Jesús, Maria y José!!* (Jesus, Mary and Joseph! – or, as Ross O'Carroll Kelly has it, JESUS MERRION JOSEPH[3]) as well as *¡Jesús mil veces!* (Jesus a thousand times, an expression of surprise) and *Sin decir Jesús* (without saying Jesus, as in *Murió sin decir Jesús* – he died suddenly). In Welsh English, the Welsh *Duw* (God) becomes the somewhat equivocally euphemistic 'Jew', as in 'Jew, there's bard [ill] he's looking!'

JASUS WEPT!

Though blasphemy has long ceased to be a capital crime or even a manner of speech of which speakers are consciously aware, the employment of euphemism is common in many Christian cultures, nominal or otherwise, and remains to some extent inherent in Dublinese. Thus the RTÉ soap *Fair City*, set in Dublin, at the outset required the common AH FOR JASUS' SAKE! to be replaced by 'Ah for James' Street sake!' – an expression never heard on the city streets. JAMES' STREET! (the home of Guinness, or UNCLE ARTHUR) is/was invariably employed simply as an expression of surprise or disbelief. The name Jesus is rendered in various other variations in the vernacular, as in the cant saying JANEY MAC ME SHIRT IS BLACK or its alternative GAWNEY MAC: 'JANEY was the respectable way of saying Jesus – or the Dublin pronunciation – JAYSUS,' Gene Kerrigan recalled of his 1950s childhood.[4] 'A totally harmless expletive was derived from this, acceptable even to nuns, let alone parents: JANEY MAC.' JAPERS; JAKERS/JAYCKERS, or simply JAY are further options. Thus the epic voyage of the *Calabar* on the Grand Canal:

> Then all became confusion, when the stormy winds did blow,
> The Bos'un slipped on an orange peel and fell into the hold below.
> The Captain cried: "Tis a pirate's brig, and on us she does gain!
> When next I sail for Clondalkin, boys, BE JAPERS I'll go by train!"[5]

Kilian Doyle found himself in Dublin's notorious Motor Taxation Office, having acquired ticket number 696 in the queue: '629. Window 7. JAYCKERS, that's merciless, I think … I'm wondering who's been shunted to the back of the queue in such a casual manner.'[6] JASUS, as Conor Goodman noted,[7] can also be used adjectivally, as in 'get OUTTA that JAYSUS garden!' Or, as Farrell in Roddy Doyle's *Brownbread* has it, 'Ah, shoot the JAYSIS Bishop an' we can all go home'.[8] Other common derivations include that employed by Vincent Caprani's old prizefighter with a grudge against journalists: 'I tried to bate the BEJASUS out of every goddam one of them — just walked straight in an' said "d'yeh work in the papers?" an' if the answer was "yes" I just fuckin'— well let fly with both fists".'[9] JASEZ BESIDE US IN ALL HARM!

INFERNAL FIRE IRONS

Other common euphemisms exhibit rather more verbal inventiveness: 'BY THE HOLY!' Maria and Richard Lovell Edgeworth observed in their essay on the Dublin shoeblack, 'is an oath in which more is meant than meets the ear; it is an ellipsis — an abridgement of an oath. The full formula runs thus — BY THE HOLY POKER OF HELL! This instrument is of Irish invention or imagination.'[10] Its shadow remained in the repertoire as simply HOLY POKER! BY THE HOLY! becoming BE THE HOKEY! as in the Dublin slang song 'De Kilmainham Minit' (c. 1788):

> He finish'd dis speech wid a sigh!
> We saw de poor fellow was sinking;
> De drizzle stole down from his eye,
> Tho' we taut he had got better spunk in.
> Wid a tip of de slang we replied [a gesture of the forefinger
>   to the nose]
> And a blinker dat nobody noted;
> De clergy stept down from his side,
> And de gabbard from under him floated;
> *Oh! BE DE HOKY,*
> It was den dat me port-royal run cold!

By the same emasculating process HOLY FATHER! becomes HOLY FARMER! or HOLY FIDDLER! Culminating in the piscine: "'HOLY MACKEREL", said Redser. "The horse falls, we're nearly KILT ...'"[11] — an example of the common devoicing of the past participle (/d/ becomes /t/), '... though not noticed by people generally and certainly not cited as typical of any types of Dublin speech, or of Dublin speech as a whole, even though they may be, the devoicing feature is far more widespread in the city than the vowel breaking is'.[12]

FATHER AND SON

Taking the name of the Lord in vain, to quote the Commandment, is also, one might hazard, 'not noticed by people generally', except when a particular usage or intonation becomes the object of popular recognition and/or derision. BEGOB/BEGOBS has virtually surrendered its divine reference: "'BE GOBS,' said he, "you're very young to be doing the BONA FIDE'"[13] (for Bona Fide in its various ramifications, see Chapter 5). If Miley's trademark HOLY GOD in the long-running RTÉ television soap, *Glenroe*, was more rural than urban, O MY GOD in all its variations has been firmly appropriated by the city, and particularly by the DORT-speaker as exemplified by the female entourage of Ross O'Carroll Kelly: 'There's hundreds of birds surrounding us at this stage, ROYSH, and all I can hear is "Oh MY God! and the odd "Oh MY God! And the occasional OH! MY! GOD![14] The usage is so prevalent amongst young women that it has given birth to a collective noun, OMIGODS. Temperate curses involving the second person of the Trinity include JESUS KATE! And JESUS TONIGHT! More explicit variations are not unknown: 'AGONISING CHRIST, wouldn't it give you a heartburn on your arse?'[15] 'Sometimes I think we underestimate ourselves in the SLAGGING stakes,' wrote Fiona Looney in a discussion of 'our ability to insult like no other nation'[16]: 'I'm not sure any other nation could have coined the phrase I COULD EAT THE HIND LEG OF THE LAMB OF GOD, although strictly speaking that's blasphemous rather than insulting'. True for you.

THEM AND US

It was easy to understand Protestants being clean. That was the difference between them and Catholics: school uniforms and clear complexions ... But if you were confused you could give a simple test: 'Which is better, the lick of a cat of the prod of a pin?' If they answered the former they were Catholic, if the latter, a Protestant.[17]

Bob Quinn's simple litmus test of half a century and more ago would scarcely do today, when perceived differences among schoolkids are more likely to centre upon colour than creed. But that was another country. In Paul Durcan's Dublin childhood, Protestants, and particularly their 'rodent-like' clergymen, were a mystery:

Our parents called them PARSONS
Which turned them from being rodents
Into black hooded crows
Evilly flapping their wings
About our virginal souls . . . .[18]

'We knew they existed, we knew they were out there, some-where, the PRODDIES,' Gene Kerrigan recalled: 'Some of the older folk might occasionally make a remark about the PRODDY-WODDIES. We'd heard of them but it went without saying that there were none of them in our neighbourhood.'[19] C.S. Andrews wrote of the First Lieutenant in his Company of the Irish Volunteers:

> Kenny had a PROTESTANT DROP in him. His mother was a Protestant blacksmith's daughter ... Perhaps it was this Protestant drop that produced in Kenny an extreme puritanism.[20]

'We always spoke of the CHAPEL', he recalled, 'never the CHURCH. The use of the phrase GOING TO CHURCH would immediately identify the speaker as a Protestant, or at least as a CASTLE CATHOLIC' (a breed that might be seen to be resurrecting itself in a new guise with the appearance of a number of Sirs in what was once known as THE CITY OF DREADFUL KNIGHTS. The Castle itself, in the era of British power, was known as the DEVIL'S HALF-ACRE). The convic-tion, according to Dominic Behan, was that 'all Protestants were rich and wore good clothes and didn't play in the streets. They were sissies, and when the fellas saw them coming over the bridge from Jones Road they used to shout PRODDIE DOG . . . .'[21]

> PRODDY WODDY BLUE-GUTS
> Never said a prayer
> Catch him by the left leg
> And throw him down the stair.
>
> CATTY, CATTY go to Mass
> Ridin' on the Divil's ass
> When the Divil rings the bell
> All good Catties go to hell.[22]

Each sect, if now to a lesser extent, cherishes its own colloquialisms, with a very few, perhaps including PRAYING MINNIES, CRAWTHUMPERS and HOLY JOES (though not SORROWFUL MYSTERIES, applied to singularly doleful individuals) crossing the sectarian divide. HOLY MARYS are also overwhelmingly Catholic:

> Anyway, this particular day in Bewley's one holy mary says to the other: "Amn't I just coming from the religious counter in Clery's where I wanted to buy a statue of the blessed Martin, and the girl hands me down this one the colour of soot? So I says to her: 'MOTHER OF GOD, I never knew he was as dark as that. Do you have anything lighter?'"[23]

In the old Latin mass, according to Éamonn MacThomáis, 'the *Domine, Christus, Sanctus*… were nicknamed into DOMINICK STREET, PATRICK STREET, CHRISTCHURCH AND THE COOMBE'.[24] The Oblate Fathers, he adds, were at one time known as the BODY SNATCHERS. Metaphor also played its part:

> There was silence again. Then Mr Power said, point-blank: 'To tell you the truth, Tom, we're going to make a retreat.' 'Yes, that's it', said Mr Cunningham, 'Jack and I and M'Coy here — we're going to WASH THE POT.'[25]

From a later, less reverent generation, a caller to the BBC radio programme *Word 4 Word* offered the contribution 'a nun is a COVERED WAGON'.[26]

TAKING THE MICHAEL

CONFO (confirmation) and HAILERS (Hail Marys), also self-evidently from the Catholic side (the sacrament of confirmation, or its public celebration, is less of a HOLY SHOW amongst PRODDIES or PRODS) exhibit the confusing Dublin deployment of the endearment suffix: -o; -er, -ie. There would seem to be no rule that regulates this usage and 'endearment', the formal term, is often given grudgingly (few came to love the now deposed CORPO, aka Dublin Corporation) while the use of the term MORTALLER — a mortal sin — is scarcely indicative of close affection. ('Yer man has a face like a plateful of mortal sins.') But as with the many Spanish diminutives, -illo, ito, -cito, -ecillo, -ezeuelo, etc., you could easily make a holy show of yourself employing the wrong one at the wrong time: the transubstantiation of Michael to MICKO, MICKSER or Mick would merit a study in itself. MICKEY, a synonym for the penis, is rarely if ever employed as a diminutive in this sense: anyone who attempted to do so would be MAKING A PIG'S MICKEY of it. 'On Moore Street a woman was buying her fruit and veg. and picked up a bunch of bananas and the trader shouts out "stop maulin' them der not mickeys ya know!"'[27] In the Dublin slang of the 1920s, a MICKEY-DAZZLER was a 'ladykiller' — both terms long since faded.

The Dublin writer, Vincent Caprani, is known as VINNIE to some friends and acquaintances, VINNO to others: 'I tell you, Vinno, I'm a walking sarcophagus of war wounds that would make the agony in the Garden of Gethsemane look like an afternoon picnic';[28] and he also appears in the same volume as the some-what less popular VINCE. The order would seem to be, in ascending progression of intimacy and acquaintance, Vince—Vinnie—Vinno ... but you wouldn't want to stake your life on it. The interplay of endearment suffixes is particularly in evidence in the sporting world, where few escape with their given names intact. Thus Mary Hannigan, in reporting the RTÉ television coverage of Ireland's exit from the World Cup,[29] featured BILLO (Bill O'Reilly), EAMO (Eamon Dunphy), LIAMO (Liam Brady) and, odd man out, GILESIE (Johnny Giles). There would equally seem to be no fixed rule as to whether the first name or the surname receives the treatment, and the bizarre effect of applying the endearment suffix to a name of Gaelic origin (Liam, Eamon, etc.) does not appear to strike anyone as incongruous.

FLIP SIDE

'"BAD CESS TO THEM." It was a dire but innocent curse cast by members of a generation that didn't indulge so easily in the colourful language that we use today,' Gene Kerrigan recalled: 'We kids used FLIP as a euphemism acceptable even in adult company. Flip it. Blow it. *In extremis*, damn it. Until we graduated — strictly among ourselves to the real thing.'[30] At about the same period, a Dublinman who would have fallen into the category of a HARD CHAW or HARD TICKET was taking a short cut down a city laneway when he met up with two individuals (male), accompanied by a CHISELLER of tender age, engaged in a strenuous verbal battle involving a quantity of colourful expletives. Your man listened to them for a few moments with growing disapproval. Finally he lit into them: 'YIS should be ashamed of YIZZER selves', sez he, 'using language like that in front of this poor innocent little fucker!'

But it probably flowed over him like water. 'Your Dublin chiseller is the salt of the earth,' claimed Leslie Daiken. 'The vision of Celt and Saxon flows in his bloodstream, and this has been bravely contaminated by a score of other toxic intakes.'[31] Echoic of chiselers are the less common OUZELERS, with an interesting, if debatable provenance. In 1685 a trading ship, the *Ouzel Galley*, left Dublin fully laden for foreign parts. Allegedly captured by pirates, nothing was heard of her until she reappeared some five years later, some of the crew discovering that in the meantime their wives had taken new husbands and acquired new children. 'Indeed to this day in Ringsend,' according to John Moran, 'it has been noted that children born in unorthodox circumstances are known as "ouzelers."'[32]

Chiselers (or chisellers) could also be KIDGERS — as sparrows are SPADGERS: '"We're leafin' the kidger here for a few seconds," said Tom's friend; "he'll just sit quiet and be in nobody's way."'[33] A pious hope, no doubt: kids, for good reason, are not always the apple of everyone's eye:

'Well, I've one up on Jem Larkin in that respect,' said Mother.
'He wasn't crucified having children anyhow.'

'He was crucified making this a better country for your
little GOD-FORBIDS!' bellowed back Father.[34]

And Killian Doyle recalled a man running over a neighbouring
kid's bicycle: '"You stupid child, look at my car!" he ranted ..." If
there's even a hint of a scratch on my paintwork, I'll LEATHER
you!"'[35] He could equally, and with the same result, have been
DUG OUT OF HIM or, verbally or physically, PUT MANNERS ON HIM.

OUT OF THE MOUTHS. . .

'Happy those early days when I/Shin'd in my angel-infancy',
lamented the poet Henry Vaughan (1622–95), but apparently it
is not like that any more ... if it ever was. 'They're starting it
younger and younger these days,' noted Conor Goodman:

> I was at least five before I heard about it. But my daughter did
> it for the first time the other night, in the back of the car, and
> she's not two years old yet. She uttered her first swear word ...
> 'F**K'S SAKE!' she bellowed.'[36] [asterisks in the original]

'The asterisk is the equivalent of the thong', suggested the journalist John Waters:

> We all know what's in there. Newspapers will publish 'f**k', but
> surely either the reader reading it will know that one asterisk is
> for 'u' and the other is for 'c', and they'll be able to spell it out
> for themselves, or else they don't know, in which case they'll
> be confused, and start thinking to themselves, oh this must be
> 'fork' or whatever. It's absurd.[37]

Absurd it may be, but the printed euphemism has, for varying reasons and with few exceptions, proved more durable than its verbal equivalent. To some, however, the practice savours of sexism. Fiona Looney suggested that 'women should reclaim the c-word. Just as homosexuals took possession of "queer" from the straight community and African-Americans now have sole rights to the word "nigger", so we should rise up and take control of c***. We have nothing to lose but our asterisks.'[38]

BROUGHT TO BOOK

'For an example of Irish fluency with the f-word,' wrote Roberta Gray, 'one need go no further than down the street — although different areas will obviously yield different results, with inner-city Dublin taking the biscuit for frequency and inventiveness.'[39] If this is so, it would seem to be, in a historical perspective, a relatively recent development. Paddy Crosbie, writing of the period 1914-1930, recalled that 'the language of the Dublin Markets Area was coarse and vulgar, but the now-famous four-letter word had not taken over the vocabulary yet.'[40] Now, the takeover is complete. Jesse Sheidlower's 'complete history of the word in all its robust and various uses'[41] virtually exhausts both subject and reader but still manages to miss what could well be original Dublinese variations: FAIR FUCKS TO HIM, the equivalent of FAIR DUES (cf. Australian 'fair goes'); (an appropriately pseudo-euphemistic variation of this usage is offered by Barry Egan: 'FAIR BALLS to him. Despite just returning from an extended honeymoon with the exquisitely beautiful Gayle Killilea, Sean Dunne still has the energy to go clubbing'[42]). Also FOR FUCK'S SAKE; a quasi-affectionate usage as in YOU LOOK FUCKIN' GORGEOUS (again cf. Australian employment of 'bastard' in a similar sense); and the cant phrase, beloved of, if not coined by, Brendan Behan: FUCK THE BEGRUDGERS. The insertion of the word or its derivatives between normally contiguous parts of speech is exemplified in Alan Roberts' Mountjoy prison novel: '"SHUT TA FUCK UP, an' get some a that inta

93

ya before the screws is around again for fall in.'"[43] (Note the plural subject with singular verb.) If the local application of the f-word and its derivatives is generally indiscriminate, a hint of precision might be observed in the application of the past participle: something that is not terminally rendered inoperative might be described as KNACKERED, whilst damaged beyond repair it is unquestionably FUCKED. (KNACKER, or CREAM CRACKER, originally a buyer of worn-out horses, refers to a member of the travelling community who, before political correctness set in, would have been called a tinker, subsequently an itinerant. It is now equally commonly a general term of abuse).

CULTURE SHOCK

Roberta Gray quotes theatre critic Karen Fricker, a Los Angeles native: 'Every single American I know who comes here is shocked by the Irish use of bad language ... Obviously the key word here is "cunt" which in Ireland just means an idiot ... Another really noticeable thing here is the use of the word "fuck" about five times in a sentence, almost as punctuation'[44] – and used, she might have added, mostly unconsciously. Typical is the anecdote of the Dub recounting ad nauseam to a captive pub audience the events of his day, each noun preceded by FUCKIN' and several other parts of speech intersected with the same adjective. Finally, 'And then what happened?' from a sufferer anxious to call a halt to the tedious narrative. 'What happened?' sez your man: 'What happened was I went home to the wife and we had sexual intercourse.' This illustrates the observable fact that the Dublin use of 'fuck' and its derivatives – FUCKIN' in particular – generally carries no direct reference to the sexual act and is employed irrespective of audience, male or female, young or old. This is paralleled, for example, in colloquial Cuban Spanish, where the equivalent word *joder* 'has completely, or almost totally, lost its accepted meaning of sexual coition.'[45] And also in popular Catalan usage which similarly substitutes *fotre* for *fer* (do) and a wide range of other verbs.[46] It is not therefore surprising that under these circumstances the word and its derivations are employed without reticence in respect of the young and putatively innocent. Thus the character Farrell in Roddy Doyle's *Brownbread*, addressing his offspring: 'I come home for me FUCKIN' dinner an' — an' I find your mammy with her nerves in FRITS ... Even the dog was THROWIN' A WOBBLER ...'[47]

'THE FUCKING PEACE PROCESS'

From Charles Haughey's legendary 1984 interview in the magazine *Hot Press* (the name is a play on what in other jurisdictions is known as an airing cupboard) to the well-documented linguistic indiscretions of contemporary figures from Bono to Sinéad O'Connor (gender distinctions no longer apply), the use of the f-word and its derivatives would seem to transcend such linguistic class boundaries as exist in, to quote Roberta Gray again, 'the Irish tendency to sprinkle our language with profanities, with no intention to offend'.[48] That there remains a lingering sense of offence, however, is instanced by the continued employment of mimetic substitutes, by far the most common of which is FECK (< Old English *feccan*, fetch, seek, gain, take, or alternatively Germ. *fegen*, plunder]. In Gene Kerrigan's childhood years, 'the euphemism FECK was widespread. It had two meanings. You could tell someone to FECK OFF; or a thief might feck something from a shop'.[49] And its usage follows in its varying forms (FECKER, etc.) the variations of what might be termed the parent word. Thus Killian Doyle:

> According to some COD-psychology ... buyers reckon having a car the colour of precious metal lends gravitas and importance and commands respect from other motorists. Which is a load of FECKOLOGY, in my eyes.[50]

DOUZE POINTS

The larger question as to why, FOR FUCK'S SAKE, the Irish in general have complemented their Eurovision achievements by being recognised as the most foul-mouthed nation in Europe is beyond the scope of this enquiry, but in spite of the casual usage of the f-word at all levels of society, there remains the belief that its employment in the public domain, and by the Dublin establishment in particular (as, for instance, former Taoiseach John Bruton's expression of exasperation at the progress of Northern negotiations) is not appropriate to high or even middle office. The prejudice is intuitive: as Roberta Gray observed, 'while it's almost presumed that any rock star worth his or her salt cannot help but issue forth a stream of profanities, politicians are expected to keep their act clean when in public'.[51] But there is an underlying dichotomy in that at the same time we expect such public figures to be no different from ourselves. As Fiona Looney explains:

> We need to take time out to remind ourselves that we are unimpressed by celebrity, underwhelmed by success and hugely entertained by shouting abuse in the street. And we should remember that after all, that's why other people have always loved the Irish. Which just goes to show what a collection of shallow international arseholes the rest of the world really is.[52]

ARTS AND PARTS

'After the number of times I SUNK THE LOG last night,' boasted Lee Dunne, 'she'd never believe I was a BROWNIE [homosexual]'.[53] If taking the word for the deed, so to speak, is a common characteristic of Dublin invective, the vocabulary to describe the sexual act itself and its associated acts are certainly not lacking. A SLICE OFF THE LEGS, A RATTLE, A BIT OF STRAY, THE BOLD THING, THE ONE THNG, A RUB OF THE RASHER, A RUB OF THE RELIC: the difficulty lies in the identification of what terms, if any, could be hazarded as Dublinese with any degree of acceptance. The website sex-lexis.com, which lists some 1,300 synonyms for penis, does not apparently include (September 2005), BURY THE BALDY FELLA as descriptive of inter-course, though it cites several phrases built upon the word 'bald'. GOOTER, also penis, is listed with the qualification that the usage is Irish: Roddy Doyle uses it, as he also uses BUGLE in a similar sense, though specifically of the erect organ, which the same website notes as 'obsolete'. These three, if only on contextual evidence, might be offered a reasonably secure Dublin domicile. But what of LANGER, another term for the same organ, also employed by Doyle, but strongly claimed as a native of Cork? Its derivatives, LANGERS, LANGERED and LANGERATED, denoting subtle gra-dations of intoxication, possibly by the analogous extension of 'pissed', certainly cannot be ceded as the exclusive property of that city. It is difficult to recall the days when the euphemism ranged supreme in this matters, if only in 'polite' intercourse: 'A bit like a film in the Classic', wrote Bob Quinn, describing a picture in the National Gallery, 'huge and plenty of blood but all the tits and things covered up with bits of clothes. You could imagine them, last thing before they died … dragging their clothes across to hide their YOKIBUSSES'.[54] (A yokibus is a somewhat more evasive form of the flexibly indefinite YOKE.)

NETHER REGIONS

Of the contingent male apparatus, MEBS, KAKS, BOLLIX, and their extended usages, as in THAT OUL' BOLLIX, a term of disapproval, have a strong Dublin pedigree, reflected, in the case of bollix, in the phonetic transcription of an otherwise common slang term. PUBIKERS (public hair) is common to both sexes. On the distaff side, Dublin females sport DIDDIES, DOLLIES or JABS on the upper part of the body, the GEE, GOWL (< Irish *gabhal,* crotch), GROWLER or RASHER, elsewhere: 'Lilly Neary has a lovely gee and her pore

Paddy got his B.A. and by the holy fly I wouldn't recommend you to ask me what class of a tree they were under when he put his hand on her and enjoyed that'.[55] The female organ in question was concealed by DRAWERS, a term, obsolete elsewhere, which persisted in Dublin into the present. To quote Molly Bloom: '... of course he's mad on the subject of drawers that's plain to be seen always SKEEZING at those brazenfaced things on the bicycles with their skirts blowing up to their navels ...'[56] There would seem to be some uncertainty amongst Dublin journalists, however, concerning what is taking its place. Thus *The Irish Times*, 24 June 1998: 'The alleged victim was crying and then went into the bathroom with her friend. Her knickers were gone even though she had gone to bed in a shirt, bra and knickers, said counsel'. And the same newspaper reporting the same case the following day: 'She told Mr Liam Reidy SC, prosecuting, she realised her panties had been removed as she slept. She had gone to bed in a shirt, bra and panties ...' One can, however, still be up and down LIKE A HOOR'S DRAWERS ON A SATURDAY NIGHT; though someone who is judged to be a walking disaster is referred to as a total HOOR'S KNICKERS.

FINE THINGS

The prevailing sexual freedom, if such it can be termed, has produced its own vocabulary relating to the rites of courtship and its conclusions: FOOLING AROUND, MEETING and SHIFTING, for example, refer to activities not quite as innocent as they sound. However, in the current conditions of both physical and verbal mobility, it is unlikely that these pastimes, or the words to describe them, can be credibly confined within the capital. An old-fashioned GOOZER or WEAR describes a kiss as if you meant it (hence to WEAR THE HEAD OFF somebody), perhaps. The participating male might be further tempted, or encouraged, to DROP THE HAND, especially if the female recipient is A FINE, GOOD or GREAT HOULT (< 'hold', in the sense of a vigorous and encompassing embrace). Similarly, 'We're referring, obviously, to the appalling attacks on both Bertie Ahern and his former SQUEEZE, Celia Larkin ....'[57] Active indulgence in such close encounters might result in a SNAPPER, brought into the world in the ROTO (the Rotunda Lying-In Hospital) or, in the RARE OUL' TIMES, by a HANDYWOMAN, an unlicensed midwife and/or a NURSE-TENDER, a hired nurse. Should one such infant follow another within the space of twelve calendar months, they were known collectively as IRISH TWINS. Exceptionally fecund mothers (seven or more) were identified in the Dublin of the 1930s and 1940s as GRAND MULTIPARAS. The last out might have been described by envious oul' wans as THE SHAKINGS OF THE BAG.

Another aspect of female sexuality — menstruation — is variously referred to: to HAVE THE PAINTERS IN; to GET ONE'S AUNT; '"No, no stop, fuck off, please, no don't, I HAVE ME FLOWERS, I have me flowers, pleassse ..."';[58] and, even more colourfully: 'One girl disappears with a youth into the gloom ... "Are they?" you ask. "No", somebody laughs. "She has a VAMPIRE'S TEABAG in"'.[59] The externally applied versions are known as JAM RAGS or BRILLO PADS.

With regard to the vocabulary of sexual orientation, Michael Parsons suggested:

> If you've been having a lie-down since the days when there was honey still for tea and 'gay' was how Maude felt when invited into the garden', you may have missed that word's torrid transmutation ... its latest use is to witheringly describe something nerdish or unfashionable. Brunch, shoe polish, Ulster loyalism and the Eurovision Song Contest are 'gay'.[60]

But if the terms for male homosexuals are not notably Dublin-specific and 'trannies' — transsexuals — are widely dispersed in the Anglophone world, LEZZERS (lesbians) are to be encountered, according to Jonathon Green,[61] only in Ireland, Australia and the USA, as in this sample of male abuse addressed to a new arrival in the RASHERHOUSE (women's wing) of THE JOY:

'Hope you got a good RIDE last night, 'cos ya won't he gettin'
much of it where you're goin".
    "Sept if ya inta fuckin' the dikes.'
    'Are ya a LEZZER, are ya but?'[62]

BRINGING UP THE REAR

After the sexual act and its parts, the process and avenue of
excretion and its surrounding areas figure largely in the vocabulary of the citizens. For a long time, RTÉ radio was markedly self-
effacing in giving credit to the composer of the signature tune
of its popular *Sunday Miscellany* programme — the name of
Samuel Scheidt (1587–1654) apparently not being considered
suitable for mention on the Sabbath. As between SHIT and SHITE,
Dublin and most of the country favour the latter; though, as in
the matter of endearment suffixes, it is difficult to categorise
the usage with any degree of conviction. Is there a sense that
SHITE is less anal-specific and therefore somewhat more genteel, if
that is the word? As in the introduction to Roddy Doyle's
Brownbread: 'It [the SFX Centre] had none of the things we
expect to see in a good theatre ... young men and women
dressed in black talking meaningful SHITE during the intermis-
sion.'[63] On the other hand, and again from Alan Roberts:

> 'It's better than hangin' round the laundry all day talkin' about
> all the great strokes we've done, or walking round in circles
> talking SHIT.'
>   'That so now? Well TALKIN' SHIT was good enough for you til
> little Miss Snotty Nose arrived.'[64]

Is the distinction in the quality or content of the talk? The sex of
the talker? Or the location: shite in the Abbey and shit in the
JOY? As with endearment suffixes, the rule would seem to be that
there is no rule. Fiona Looney, on a visit to Newry, acquired 'a

quantity of wine for which I believe the technical term is A SHIT-LOAD'.[65] To consume with shite and onions? And the noun itself, in that latter form at least, can be applied metonymically: 'We all fell around the place — and fair play to the girls because they BROKE THEIR SHITES laughing'.[66]

TURNING THE OTHER CHEEK

ARSE and its derivatives draw much of their expressive power from what the eighteenth-century French phonologist, J. Mather Flint, called the 'extrèmement rude' Irish pronunciation of the letter /r/ compared with the 'presque muette' /r/ of the English. According to Joan Beal, comparing the received pronunciation with those of Scotland and Ireland, 'since loss of /r/ was actually stigmatised, there was no incentive for the "polite" speakers of Dublin or Edinburgh to adopt this sound change'.[67] Hence the consonant's continuing vigour among both polite and less polite Dublin speakers in words and phrases such as ARSEWAYS (backwards), ARSE OVER KICK (head over heels), ASK ME ARSE, already cited, and the almost-obsolete acronym KMRIA, deriving from the august membership of the Royal Irish Academy. Thus Myles Crawford in James Joyce's Ulysses: 'He can KISS MY ROYAL IRISH ARSE ... Any time he likes, tell him.'[68] On the other hand, a less confrontational Crawford might have decided 'NOT TO BOTHER ME ARSE about him', that HE DIDN'T KNOW HIS ARSE FROM HIS ELBOW or have claimed that he knew him when HE HADN'T AN ARSE TO HIS TROUSERS. KMRIA finds its equivalent in Irish in póg mo thon, literally 'kiss my arse', from which emanates the following by Flann O'Brien: '"It is the parents I pity, the suffering parents that brought them up wearing their fingers to the bone and going without nourishing food in their old age to give the young POGUEMAHONES an education"'.[69] Brendan Behan, no mean speaker and writer of Irish himself, was wont to refer to those sporting the fáinne, the gold ring confirming fluency in the language, as ERSEHOLES.

BULLS' LOOKS

Though contemporary terms employed in the business of EFFING AND BLINDING are generally succinct in form, there are still several overtly offensive Dublin expressions that roll more lingeringly off the tongue. When, at the count in Ballsbridge, Una Bean Mhic Mhathúna came up with the intriguing WIFE-SWAPPING SODOMITES (who does what and with what and to whom?) with which to lacerate the advocates of a 'yes' vote in the 1996 divorce referendum, the phrase seemed destined for a brief if colourful currency. But there it was, apparently alive and well seven years later, in the word-hoard of journalist Fintan O'Toole: 'though he won't thank us for it, some of the credit for Archbishop Martin's appointment has to go to those of us on the wife-swapping sodomite wing of Irish life.'[70] The Dubliner who is BLACK OUT WITH somebody and about to WOOL/EAT THE HEAD OFF him or her will, however, tend to express him- or herself in words of a maximum of two syllables. This area of confrontational vocabulary is subject to more rapid change than many another, with a substantial and increasing percentage of imports, but happily many traditional terms remain in the repertoire. 'Why does it have to be me, Mister T', complained Eamonn MacThomáis' ailing interlocutor, 'like ya know like I'm no BOWSIE, GURRIER or GOWGER. I take care of me health like.'[71] Note, in passing, the generic MISTER T. The Dublin habit of reducing the surname to an initial is said to derive from ancient pub practice, the barman referring thus to a habitual customer on the premises in case an irate phone call from HERSELF might result in his presence being betrayed. Joyce deploys it in *Dubliners*:

'About that little matter I was speaking to you about ...'
   'That'll be all right, MR. H.', he said. 'Yerra, sure the little HOP-O'-MY-THUMB has forgotten all about it.'[72]

Bowsie, to return to the matter in hand, is another of those

words of debatable etymology (< Germ. *böse*, bad, evil, mali-
cious, or < Mid. Eng. *bousen*, to drink to excess – in Hiberno-
English, the two senses not infrequently meet). Again, this is a
word which projects itself in various directions: one may BOWSEY
AROUND; 'Mr Manning,' according to Roddy Doyle, 'handed out the
punishments for BLAGARDISM [*sic*] and BOWSIEISM, or for gross
neglect of lessons.'[73] Of other terms of opprobrium, SPOON, dating
from the late eighteenth century and originally connoting a fool
or simpleton, has acquired more of an edge in the Dublin vernacular: 'Your dad's a MAD SPOON, Ao.'[74] And Ao supplies another:
'Good Jesus! He's a fuckin' LOOPER.' Watching Formula One races,
in the opinion of Lise Hand, 'has little to do with admiration of
the cars and more to do with admiration of the twenty-odd
loopers who are all trying to round a narrow corner at the same
time ...'[75] LOOPER derives from 1920s UK slang *loopy*, eccentric or
crazy, and again the –*er* suffix is typical: compare New Zealand
slang *loopy*, a tourist, apparently from the habit of asking the
natives stupid questions. This universally ambivalent attitude
towards the foreign cash-cow is reflected in the contemptuous
Hiberno-English pronunciation of *tourist*, the first syllable – *tou*
– rhymed with *now*.

HAVING THEIR BLING

But the repertoire of expletive abuse is almost endless. GET, or,
more viscerally Dublin, GIT, couples simple malediction with a
strong dose of contempt: 'The DA advanced slowly, snarling
through gritted teeth: "Get out of this yard, you snotty-nosed
oul' git"'.[76] Killian Doyle, writing of the vogue in Britain for the
term *chav*, observed that

> ... in case you think we've escaped, the chav mindset is over
> here too. Except that we call them SCOBIES or SCUMBAGS. (To be
> fair, a scumbag is actually an extreme form of the species, a

type of *ünter*-chav, if you will. A chav will scrape your car with his sovereign ring out of spite as he walks past, whereas a scumbag will just steal it.)[77]

In this matter of name calling or generally GIVING OUT STINK, even Ross O'Carroll Kelly has something to learn from his precocious offspring:

He ended up getting J-LOED, which was a new one on me. 'It means Juvenile Let Off, you fucken PLANK', he goes to me on the phone from outside the cop shop'.[78]

(To be PLANKING IT is to be in a nervous condition). And the same character (father, not son) defines a SCOBIE — or SKOBIE — as a Dublin 'chav': 'Wearing sports wear as clothes. Jewellery on men. Facial hair on men. And women. Call football BALL'. There are other views on the localisation of 'chav', however: The BBC radio programme *Word 4 Word* of 3 August 2005, as reported by Pat Stacey, asked 'how you describe young men and women who wear brand-label tracksuits, Burberry baseball caps and scarves, and lots of cheap, garish bling jewellery'.[79] The question prompted the response from a listener: 'we have a very specific word for this in Dublin ... We call them SKANGERS'. Eoghan Rice quoted the online dictionary *Wikipedia*:

Among the indigenous identifying features of the skanger is a high-pitched tone and a difficulty in pronouncing vowel-sounds. 'A common greeting used by so-called skangers is pronounced STARRY BUD?, a corruption of the Dublin phrase WHAT'S THE STORY, BUD?, meaning "how are you, my friend?"'[80]

Rice defines another term of abuse, SCONER, as an 'insult for northsiders coming from the phrase MAD SCONE used by wannabe scumbags'. The latter definition is surely an oxymoron: to want to be and to become a scumbag is surely one and the same thing? In the context of most references, both skangers and sconers would appear to be predominantly male. SKREGEENS, however, would seem to be exclusively of the female sex:

> ... when he got to the GPO a gang of HEADERS came round from Henry Street. 'Oh fuck', my friend said to himself, it was too late to cross the road. Then just as he was about to get away with it, he notices one of the skregeens in the group was pretty cute ...[81]

HEAD CASES

A HEAD is simply a friend or colleague, as in the greeting HOWYA HEAD! but a HEADER is a dangerously unbalanced individual, invariably male, and to LOSE THE HEAD is to find oneself in that condition. A HEAD-THE-BALL is perhaps more to be derided than feared, as is a THOOLERMAWN (cf. Ir. *tuathalán,* blunderer, tactless person) together with his (always his) mirror-images, the THULLABAWN and the LOODERAMAWN: Mr Collopy doesn't think very much of 'young thullabawns of fellows got out in baggy drawers playing this new golf out beyond on the Bull Island ... Well, HOW ARE YOU? We're as fit for Home Rule here as the blue men in Africa we are to judge by those Bull Island looderamawns'.[82] If one might suspect Flann O'Brien/Myles na gCopaleen of importing the two latter derogatory designations from somewhere beyond the Pale, there is no doubting the urban authenticity of the expostulatory HOW ARE YOU? with the characteristic emphasis on the verb. (One is left to wonder how and why the communications company in question came up with the slogan: 'Vodafone – how are you?')

A LATCHICO – again exclusively of the male sex – is another of those Dublin designations concerning which there is a continuing disagreement as to origin and even application. Vincent Caprani suggests that it is Dockland slang for a waster or a rogue,[83] but it may also connote someone who is evidently NOT THE FULL SHILLING. To quote Myles again: 'The brother takes a very poor view of the Labour Party CAWBOGUES he calls them. And what else are they? *I don't know.*'[84]

The MESSER, like the GOM or GAWM, is always with us, a danger to organised society, if only through eejity incompetence, relied upon to MAKE A BAGS of whatever he — usually he — undertakes. An OUL' BAGS is a thoroughly despicable individual; similarly in the case of a SLEEVEN, there is a degree of malice aforethought mixed with mere native cunning, the original Irish *slibhín* connoting a sly, wily individual. Far less confrontational, if tediously complaining, is an UNCLE PAYTHER, from the character Peter Flynn in O'Casey's *The Plough and the Stars*; whilst an OLD SEGOTIA could most likely be addressed without offence as MISTER-ME-FRIEND. Right? RIGHT? (Dortspeak ROYSH?) — a handy rhetorical interrogation — is effectively a concise version of KNOW WHAT I MEAN? Thus Myles na gCopaleen, yet again:

> Now say there's some ould one down the road laid up with a bad knee. Right. She sends for the doctor. Right. But where are you in the meantime? You're laid up, too. You're inside in your bed with a bad cold. Right. You send for the doctor, too. Right . ....[85]

GRAND STAND

Nothing dates as fast as the expression of enthusiastic approval or disapproval. Happily the tedious and ubiquitous 'cool' has no place in a catechism of *echt* Dublinese, which can still boast a few of its own superlatives, and vice versa, even if some are a little faded:

> Some years ago a little woman was in Bewley's in Westmoreland Street, hammering into a grandiose éclair, when she suddenly declared: 'Isn't it SAVAGE to think that a place like this is always in danger of closing down?'[86]

More recently the negative/positive polarisation has undergone a radical reversal: 'Paddy Hallanan, a patient, straight-talking Dub with a sense of humour, is a huge hit with the children. They tell him he's DEADLY several times.'[87] This is frequently modified as BLEEDIN' DEADLY. Michael Parsons observed that 'there are some gentlefolk for whom "wickedness" involves a small amontillado before Sunday lunch. But for most young people alcohol in more copious quantities is WICKED — as in very good and highly desirable'.[88] RAPID carries a similar, if unreversed, meaning. Rather less enthusiastic — though almost infinitely adjustable — is the appealingly anomalous GRAND. According to Ross Golden-Bannon,

> ... it can mean anything from 'that's extra, double, super fantastic' to 'I'm only just ok but could be borderline bi-polar given half the chance' to 'we made do with it but we weren't best pleased', it's all in the intonation.[89]

Also dependent upon the intonation is BRUTAL, not quite as condemnatory as it sounds but pronounced with a prominent glottal stop (bru'al) for maximum effect.

There are, of course, less equivocal expressions of displeasure and disbelief, approval or disapproval: ME ELBOW! — where the arm euphemistically substitutes for the arse; 'when I say that we left the Chameleon [a restaurant in Temple Bar] without finishing our meal,' confided Tom Doorley, 'you could be forgiven for thinking that the whole experience was NOT UP TO SNUFF.'[90] For Dermot Bolger, 'it was a SCUTTERY evening in Autumn. The concrete in Maggie's backyard was glistening after squalls of rain.'[91] But perhaps 'scuttery' is more to do with climate than generalised carping. Of wider application, and characterising anything from a mild inconvenience to a full-blown disaster is the expressive adjective WOJUS; it might also, if not too serious, be a LEMONER.

They come and go, fall in and out of favour, but those that are truly racy of the soil — if a culchie image may be hazarded —

have a life of their own, particularly if they inhabit that territory on the verge of the equivocal. Writing of her younger years, Fiona Looney confessed, 'another word I loved back then was GNICK. Roddy Doyle has a passage in *The Van* when Jimmy Rabbitte is in a posh restaurant and the waiter gives him the wine to taste. "Very gnick", says he … One of the reasons I liked gnick was because it was a very Dublin thing.'[92]

5

40 PACES FROM
O'CONNELL BRIDGE

Where's the lovely Sally O'Brien and the way she might look at you? Apparently she's long gone and replaced by Miroslava, from the Czech Republic, who works in a call centre.

Michael Parsons, The Irish Times, *7 March 2005*

It is a ghostly gathering that assembles in front of the long-vanished McBirney's, '40 paces from O'Connell Bridge' on Burgh Quay. There is Sally O'Brien, of course, the subject of some serious investigative attention from Jim Figgerty. Uncle Arthur is having a quiet word with McHugh Himself and Old Mister Brennan, whilst keeping an admonitory eye on the youthful antics of Don 'n' Nelly, who are engaged in some kind of confrontation with Barney and Beaney ...

'Jim Figgerty came to town around 1969', Paul Flynn remembered.[1] 'I know this, having confirmed it with my accomplices, my sisters. For those of you not in the know, he's the man who put the figs into the fig rolls, a very pertinent question at that time.' Fig Rolls were produced by the long-established biscuit firm of Jacob's, which was responsible for an equally popular trio of comestibles. Frank McNally's '2004 Brain Teaser'[2] contained the question:

The British Home Secretary, David Blunkett, was forced to
resign after having an affair with a woman called:

(a) Coconut Creams
(b) Mikado
(c) Kimberley

Sally O'Brien, pulchritudinous protagonist of a Harp Lager television commercial, had a Dublin pub named after her; Uncle
Arthur has, of course, been around since he opened his James'
Street brewery in 1759; while the only half-fictional McHugh
Himself was long resident in a bicycle shop at the bottom of
Talbot Street. Old Mister Brennan, an excruciatingly tedious
baker, is a relative newcomer in this company. 'No offence to his
bread,' wrote the same Frank McNally, 'but I think old Mr B is
several slices short of a full loaf. It isn't even Mr Brennan who
does the ads. It's a pal of his, an unnamed sidekick (probably
called JOXER) who finds Mr B's conversation so witty he insists on
sharing it with us ...'[3] Meanwhile, the bow-tied and behatted
Barney and Beaney did the same job for Batchelor's Baked
Beans, one side-effect of their efforts being that Bachelor's Walk
was commonly mis-spelt.

Don 'n' Nelly, diminutive promoters of Donnelly's Skinless
Sausages (made in Cork Street) in the late 1950s and early
1960s, once had their names in lights not 40 paces from
McBirney's emporium:

It's true they're the talk of the nation,
They're a sausage excitingly new,
So new they are still a sensation —
And Donnelly's make them for you!

Donnelly's entered the popular musical repertoire with a radio
jingle, which concluded:

So the next time you visit your grocer
Tell him no other sausage will do;
To his other suggestions say 'No, Sir!'
It's Donnelly's ... Sausages for you!

It was said that the perceived implications of the 'other suggestions' resulted in the responsible advertising agency sustaining a well-directed BELT OF A CROZIER; or, somewhat less aggressively: 'He [Michael McDowell] did not fear "the BANG OF A CROZIER from any direction", he told the Dáil ...';[4] and even more mildly: 'In spite of, or partly because of, who knows — the occasional BAT OF A CROZIER, telly in Ireland went from strength to strength'.[5] (A BELT is also a generous intake of drink. On the way to a greyhound racecourse, Brendan Behan and two companions 'had a couple of belts before leaving Dublin and on the way out were in tolerably good humour'.[6] DEFFO!)

SIGNS OF THE TIMES

The osmosis between Dublin's industries, their products and promotions, and the language of its citizens dates at least from the eighteenth century when, as Samuel A. Ossory Fitzpatrick observed:

Each place of business was known by the name of its sign, many of them very quaint and amusing: such as the DOVE AND PENDANTS, where fans were sold; the GOAT AND MONKEY, a music-shop; the EAGLE AND CHILD, the house of a chimney sweep; the HEN AND CHICKENS, a stay-maker's; while the TEA TUB in Stephen's Street was a milliner's, and the ROYAL LEG and ROYAL STOCKING were rivals for the sale of hosiery. Provisions were commonly purchased in the public markets, of which there were several. These were attended by PENNY PORTERS, who carried home the buyer's purchases for a small fee.[7]

Trade was encouraged by a PLUCKER-IN stationed outside the premises. Printers and publishers (frequently, in that century, one and the same) operated under a number of colourful trade names and insignia: ADDISON'S HEAD; THE ANGEL AND BIBLE; THE BIBLE AND CROWN; THE BIBLE AND MITRE; THE BLUE BIBLE; FAULKNER'S HEAD (George Faulkner, Swift's publisher, was 'the Prince of Dublin Printers'); THE GLOBE AND SCALES; THE GOLDEN KEY; SIR ISAAC NEWTON'S HEAD; DR HAY'S HEAD (< a Scottish bishop); SANCHO'S HEAD (Andrew Ferrara in Bribery Lane, 1772 — perhaps a Spanish connection); SHAKESPEARE'S HEAD; THE THREE NAGS' HEAD and many others.

GREAT GAS

The commercial contribution to the vernacular continued as industry developed through the course of the following century. T.P. & R. Goodbody opened their tobacco factory in Tullamore, County Offaly, in 1843, one of their first products selling under the brand name 'Irish Roll'. Pipe smokers (cigarettes came later) considered the tobacco at the centre of the roll to be the most desirable, giving rise to the commendatory expression 'the heart of the roll', which became, in the phonetic transcription of Dublin speech, THE HEART OF THE ROUL/ROWL: 'Johnny was the heart of the rowl with vanmen and messengers, especially when they found out he could curse with the worst of them.'[8] Another century or so later, the financially challenged cigarette-smoker resorted, as did Éamonn MacThomáis, to 'Woodbines, butts and STABBERS' (the remains of a cigarette stubbed out and relit), or, in really bad times, with butts retrieved from the CHANNEL, or gutter: 'We had to fall back on the old CHANNEL FLAKE. Do you remember the gent who used to walk down Grafton Street with a pin sticking out of the end of his umbrella and he picking up the Channel Flake and cigar butts?'[9]

JAM SESSION

James Joyce concluded his valedictory diatribe, 'Gas from a Burner' (1912):

> Shite and onions! Do you think I'll print
> The name of the Wellington Monument,
> Sydney Parade and the Sandymount tram,
> Downes's cakeshop and Williams's Jam?

But of course he did: like Kipling's cat, 'he walked by himself and all places were alike to him'. *Ulysses* brims with loving commercial reference, the warp and weft of Dublin's 1904 daily life. What was that life, indeed, without Plumtree's Potted Meat — Incomplete! 'The gentle art of advertisement', as Professor MacHugh described it in *Ulysses,* appeared in that book in many guises. The Dublin Bakery Company, known to Dubliners as the DBC: 'We call it DBC because they have damn bad cakes'; 'Mr Bloom stood at the corner, his eyes wandering over the multi-coloured hoardings. Cantrell and Cochrane's Ginger Ale (Aromatic) ...' As a near-contemporary ad described it: 'The Champagne of Ireland. There is an exhilarating thrill, a delicious crispness about "C & C" Ginger Ale which imparts to it the very life and zest of champagne without the fire'.[10] Unusually Joyce does not specify the brand of soap — 'sweet lemony wax' — purchased by Bloom at Sweeny's in Lincoln Place, but it might well have been Velka, made by John Barrington & Sons at King's Inns Soap Works: '... Toilet, Violet, Nursery, Coal Tar and Sulphur Soaps, each handsomely wrapped ... pure and fragrant'.[11] On the other hand, Bloom reads with care the labels in the window of the Belfast and Oriental Tea Company in Westland Row, relishing the opulent adjectives: 'choice blend, finest quality, family tea ... made of the finest Ceylon brands.' All authentic 1904 Dublin — with one odd exception: 'the pork butcher Dlugacz who sells Bloom the kidney for Molly's breakfast ... Dlugacz was a pupil of Joyce in Trieste ... the Dlugacz reference in *Ulysses* was intended as one of Joyce's private jokes'.[12]

PIPE DREAMS

Mr Toner, in common with thousands of Dubliners like him, worked in Guinness' brewery. He was a cooper but, when his eyesight failed, he became a SMELLER: 'a man who went round sniffing at returned casks to make sure they were sweet enough to put fresh stout in'.[13] Finbarr Flood, a former employee, worked at the SCALD BANK, where this unpleasant task was undertaken and the casks cleaned[2], Mr Toner found consolation in the pipe: 'It was a Petersen's [*sic*] of course. "THE THINKING MAN SMOKES A PETERSEN PIPE", he exhaled contentedly.' Peterson was just one of the brand names which, with their attendant slogans, passed into popular use. A KINGSTON SHIRT MAKES ALL THE DIFFERENCE. The Urney chocolate factory was in Tallaght, then a remote suburb. Eamonn MacIntyre recalled:

> Mr Gay Byrne's first broadcast words were for Urney chocolate on its sponsored programme. As he says in his autobiography, 'In those days people used to shout across the street ANY TIME IS URNEY TIME'.[14]

'Each weekend,' Gene Kerrigan recalled, 'newspaper advertisements told us that "IT'S SATURDAY — DON'T FORGET YOUR LEMON'S PURE SWEETS"'.[15] Hugh Oram wrote, 'Throughout the 1940s, Lemon's pure sweets advertisements were as much a feature of *The Irish Times* on Saturdays as those for O'Dearest mattresses'.[16] The latter, with their topical limericks partnered by witty line illustrations by the cartoonist Warner, became a cult:

> Though under my window they sat,
> Singing 'Male Voice Arrangement for Cat',

> The quartet was free
> Of reaction from me —
> They can thank my ODEAREST for that!

Or, more topically, marking the first space flight:

> As onward his capsule is hurled
> This spaceman in comfort is curled.
> Confirming once more
> What was known long before,
> That ODEAREST is 'out of this world'!

The principal newspapers, though printed and published in Dublin (with the exception of the *Cork Examiner*), were national in circulation. As far as the capital was concerned, *The Irish Times* was simply the 'Times' (except when it was THE OLD LADY OF WESTMORELAND STREET — its longest-lasting abode); the *Irish Press* 'the Press'; but the *Irish Independent* was and is THE INDO and its Sunday equivalent the SINDO. 'The city streets in the early decades were filled with 'the loud cries of the bare-footed newspaper boys as they raced along with their bundles under their arm shouting BUFF MAIL OR HERAL', EVENIN' HEGAL' OR MAIL ....'[17] ('He walked along quickly through the November twilight... the fringe of the buff *Mail* peeping out of a side-pocket of his tight reefer overcoat.'[18]) The *Herald* and *Mail* were joined by the *Evening Press* in the mid-1950s. This presented the young street sellers with a problem, elucidated in one of Neil O'Kennedy's *By-Line* cartoons which appeared regularly in *The Irish Times*. One urchin, papers under his arm, explains to another, similarly furnished, that if you are Fianna Fáil, it's PRESSHEGGLERMAIL! but HEGGLEMAILERPRESS! if you're Inter-Party.

EMERGENCY RATIONS

O'Dea & Co. of Stafford Street, manufacturers of Odearest, was just one of the independent merchants which flourished before the days of multinational takeovers. 'Yes, we had umbrella merchants, clock merchants,' recalled Éamonn MacThomáis, 'but what about a gas merchant? "You're a GAS MERCHANT" meant that you were terribly funny.'[19] Humour also underscored the attribution of the regularly orbiting DUFFY'S CIRCUS as a paradigm for anything perceived to be in colourful disorder, or worse. (The Fianna Fáil government of the 1930s and 1940s, led by Éamon de Valera, was satirised as DEVVY'S CIRCUS.) Thus the Bawd in Brendan Behan's *Richard's Cork Leg*: 'A one night stand, like Duffy's Circus.'[20] In the commercial field, as elsewhere, pronunciation did not always follow accepted rules. Gateaux Cakes, in spite of the phonetic orthodoxy adhered to in the sponsored radio programme, were invariably spoken of as GAYTOX. The SWASTIKA LAUNDRY, which carried its stress on the penultimate syllable, was the source of some confusion during the course of the Emergency, as no doubt it would have been to any German pilot who happened to sight the symbol on its chimneys. At the end of that war, demobilised American soldiers, and the chewing gum they invariably carried with them, were a welcome novelty in Dublin. One of them, Corporal Edmund Antrobus, recorded his impressions in *Yank*, the monthly magazine of the US Army:

> About two weeks after the first Americans arrived, a strange distortion of an old battle cry was heard in Dublin. 'Have you got any GUMCHUM, sir', the kids asked. They thought that gum and chum were two syllables of the same word. Some old people in Dublin have somehow interpreted the 'gum, chum' expression as something you say in America instead of 'How do you do?'[21]

Visiting Yanks were equally in demand among the female population. Neighbours of a Mrs Healion, according to Bob Quinn, 'hinted darkly that she should have no difficulty getting real nylons from visiting sailors because she wore Clery's knickers which had the slogan ONE YANK AND THEY'RE DOWN printed on them.'[22] A popular street cry, addressed only half in jest to any fanciable female and relating to the happy era before the advent of tights made the procedure that much more demanding, was GET THEM ORF YA! Happily the invitation still stands, if one is to believe Nuala O'Faolain, writing of the British mammary 'celebrity': '... the first thing anyone will notice about Jordan is her breasts. First, last and only thing, actually, if you're the get-'em-off-ya type of man.'[23]

HEADS OR HARPS?

'Why, my lard, as I was going past the Royal Exchange I meets Billy — "Billy", says I, "will you sky a copper?" "Done", says he — "Done", says I — and done and done's enough between two jantlemen. With that I ranged them fair and even with my HOOK-EM-SNIVEY — up they go. "MUSIC" says he — "SKULL!" says I — and down they come three brown mazards.'

This account by the Edgeworths[24] of an eighteenth-century pred-ecessor of the Australian game of two-up serves to draw attention to the fact that Dublin slang has been consistently concerned with money and its employment. The authors are duly apprecia-tive of the display of verbal invention:

To SKY is a new verb, which none but a master hand could have coined; a more splendid metonymy could not be applied upon a more trivial occasion; the lofty idea of raising a metal to the skies, is substituted for the mean thought of tossing up a halfpenny.

The HOOK-EM-SNIVEY they describe as 'an indescribable, though simple, machine, employed by boys in playing at HEAD AND HARP ...

on one side of an Irish halfpenny there is a harp; this is expressed by the general term MUSIC, which is finely contrasted with the word SKULL.' MAZARD, as the Edgeworth father and daughter add, is 'from the vocabulary of Shakespeare'. The individual whose role it was to sky the coins became known in time as the TOSSER, a term transferred to low-value coinage itself, invariably in the negative, as in the lament 'I HAVEN'T A TOSSER!'.

Heads and harps were usurped by British heads and tails — the harp was removed from the Irish coinage in 1823 — to revert again in 1928, following independence, to harps backed by the heads of sundry species of livestock. These innovative coins also carried new designations in Irish which, however, failed to pass to any serious degree into the vernacular. The French writer, Raymond Queneau, in his novel *Journal Intime* set in a surreal early 1930s Dublin, has a little innocent fun with this:

> *Il fouilla dans sa poche: il ne lui restait qu'un raol. Mrs Killarney possédait encore trois pingins. Mary avait dans son sac un florin, et moi à peu près trois punts, mais je ne montrai que deux coroins.* [He searched his pocket: all he had left was a sixpence. Mrs Killarney still had three pennies. Mary had a florin in her bag, and I almost three pounds, but I showed them only two crowns.][25]

Of all these denominations, only PUNT ever achieved anything like common acceptance, and that was only after the break with sterling made it at times convenient to use it to distinguish between the two currencies. And, of course, there never was, in modern times, a *coróin* or crown.

ISSUING THE FUDGES

DUBLIN MONEY was the popular name of the silver crown and half-crown issued in 1642 and again in 1649. King James II established mints at Dublin and Limerick in 1689, and issued what was commonly known as GUNMONEY, since it was struck from old cannon, church bells and other scrap brass and base metal. In the following century, 'it having been many years since copper half-pence or farthings were last coined in this Kingdom,' wrote Jonathan Swift,[26] 'they have been for some time very scarce, and many counterfeits passed about under the name of RAPS ... .' The name, according to Jonathon Green,[27] derives from the image of an eagle on a German coin, so badly executed that it looked more like a raven, though how it came to be circulating in Dublin is not clear. Hence, however, the expression I DON'T GIVE A RAP — I don't care at all; or, as the French put it more strongly, *je m'en fous*. By the nineteenth century, the city had acquired a comprehensively vernacular monetary nomenclature. Until 5 January 1826, the Irish currency exchanged with the British at the rate of 13 pence to the shilling, hence the term THIRTEEN or THIRTEENER; in other respects, it referred to an 'Irish dozen', as the following somewhat dismaying advertisement illustrates:

> The adoption of the English practice by the Wine Merchants of this City of delivering only 12 bottles to the dozen of all wines will take place on the 6th inst.[28]

TO COIN A PHRASE

Money in general was GOYNO or GUINO; loose change ODDS or ODJINS. A RED was the local abbreviation for the US 'red cent', an inconsequential amount: 'Had he had anything, Johnny would have given it to him; but he hadn't a red.'[29] A set of tables not taught in schools ran:

2 FUDGES	=	1 MAKE, or CAMACK [2 farthings = 1 halfpenny]
2 makes	=	1 WING [2 halfpennies = 1 penny]
2 wings	=	1 DEUCE/JUICE [2 pennies = twopence — not a coin]

3 deuces = 1 KICK [3 twopences = sixpence]
2 kicks = 1 BAR [2 sixpences = 1 shilling]

'Ara, g'on ower that,' said the jarvey, grinning, 'you've got a
JUICE left surely — deep down in th' oul' pocket, wha'?'
'Honest to God — not as much as a MAKE!'[30]

The origin of some of these names is obscure, CAMAC or CAMACK
apparently deriving, for example, from a copper coin issued by
an Arklow mining company of that name. About 1800, a humorous periodical, *The Pimlico Parliamentary Reporter*, was sold for
FOUR CAMACKS. Some names remained in limited circulation until
the advent of decimal currency in 1971, and phrases and idioms
associated with the old money in many instances survived
longer. (It should be observed, however, that the mandatory
response when offered a second drink, A BIRD NEVER FLEW ON WAN
WING, is an avian rather than a pecuniary reference, though 'we
believed growing up in Dublin,' wrote Eoin Bairéad, 'that a "wing"
was so called because it had a hen in it!'[31]) Otherwise, FARTHING
FACE, used of children, denoted a pinched, wan look; the HALFPENNY
PLACE remains an undesirable location — 'Where have you a man
now at the bar like those fellows, like Whiteside, like Isaac Butt ...
Ah! Bloody nonsense! Only in the halfpenny place!'[32] Someone
with kangaroos in the top paddock is still stigmatised as being
NOT THE FULL SHILLING:

... anywhere you looked a teddy looked back. She brought
them into the conversation — if I made a joke, she looked to
see if teddy was amused ... When she littered the flat with
half-opened tins of food for teddies, I realised she was not the
full shilling.'[33]

Other phrases, such as THE SAME OLD SIX AND EIGHTPENCE (6s 8d, as a
third of an old pound, was a commonly used denomination) have

long vanished, even if pounds, shillings and pence, individually and as a phrase, still linger on the tongue. A half-crown was TWO AND A KICK; the penny was also known as the DEE (< the lower-case letter representing Latin *denarius*, originally a Roman silver coin): '"Rot you", said Belaqua. "I'll take two. How much is that?" "Four dee", she said. Belaqua gave her a sixpence.'[34] Deuce was often written JUICE: 'The softy I am, you know, I'd ha' lent him me last juice!'[35] More generally, Orna Mulcahy wrote that a certain individual 'was even spotted the other day, foot on the rail, accepting a drink from a widowed lady who everyone knows hasn't a BRASSER'.[36] The origin is, with echoes of Swift, the brass farthing, a nugatory amount; but brasser is more usually in Dublinese a woman of easy virtue, as they used to say, or a con-temptible individual of either sex or none.

ARF ARF

One of Tom Corkery's characters looks for a loan: 'Is that all right wud yew now John — I mean y'are CARRYIN' ...'[37] For those fortunate enough to be carrying, a BRICK (£10 in old money) might have been familiar, though it would seem to have applied, more mod-estly, to the single pound note as well. The word was originally employed, in betting circles, to the pre-decimal Australian £10 note and represents, perhaps, one of the few pre-*Neighbours* antipodean importations. '... I was twenty brick to the good an' goin' out the gate before the last race an' up comes bleedin' Skinnier an' gives me this bleedin' oul' BOWLER [rhymes with *fouler*] for the last.'[38] A bowler is a dog or an ill-favoured individ-ual. In this case, the misfortunate greyhound referred to might have been better advised to join the rest of Dublin's highly knowledgeable DOGS IN THE STREET. (These canines began, in fact, as culchie dogs ON the street, that location referring to the level ground surrounding a rural dwelling). In the monetary context, Tom Corkery also recalled:

> In that leisurely and hospitable decade [1950s] a shrewd BALL-MAN could borrow a two-shilling piece (his ENTRANCE MONEY as he would call it) and entering a pub could reasonably hope ... to spend the evening as the guest of his peers.[39]

Today, he would need enough bricks to build a half-decent wall. A variation on entrance money was that required by a Dublin-based retail chain before it would agree to place a product on sale. HELLO MONEY was known, in the vernacular, as HOW-A'-YA-MONEY. The Dublin retail grocery trade was also responsible in the 1980s for a range of cheap products which, dubbed yellowpacks from their packaging style, became the metaphor for anything deemed inferior. 'Our members feel the redundancy package was a YELLOW PACK offer, and it is notably worse than most redundancy deals in the food, drink and tobacco sector.'[40]

HOWYA or HOWYEH, plural HOWAYIS or HOWYIS, the common Dublin greeting, is in some circles felt to be just that — 'common':

> But I said Hello and not Howyeh. All mothers said that their sons' girlfriends were common ... I was smiling crooked but I made sure I said Hello instead of Howyeh.[41]

However, 'saying hello to Stephen Rooney when there was anyone around was like having your skirt blown up and your knickers shown off to everyone; it was an instant REDNER and it lasted longer.'[42] The noun-form HOWYA is, by extension, applied to a generic Dubliner. The exposure of Hello money was something of a redner, or REDDENER (blush of embarrassment) for the supermarket concerned. Anyone — more usually a girl — suffering from such an affliction describes herself as SCARLET. Or: 'at breakfast at work this morning, a girl was telling how embarrassed she was when she fell over: "I was bleedin' SCARLIFIED for meself".'[43] Hello money was partnered by GOODBYE MONEY, payment exacted by members of the travelling community in return for agreeing to vacate an illegally occupied site.

JESUS SAVES

It was the custom in Dublin, particularly after a wedding, to throw a handful or two of small change for which the CHILDER would scramble: this was known as GRUSH or GRUSHIE (noun and verb): 'We stood outside and waited for the happy couple and then we started shouting "Grushie! Grushie!" Eventually the best man would throw a handful of change in the air ....'[44] In these days of credit cards and banks falling over themselves to give you money, it is difficult to imagine the era when many things were painfully acquired, instalment by instalment, on the 'hire purchase'. This was known popularly — unpopularly might be more appropriate — as the KATHLEEN MAVOURNEEN SYSTEM, after the line in Julia Crawford's 1830s ballad: '... it may be for years and it may be forever'. Others, particularly hard-pressed wives, relied on the DIDDLEY/DIDDLY/DIDLEY clubs — the poor man's Credit Union: '... No but lissen John I'm tarrible grateful for them readies the missus'll have a few bar comin' outa the diddly when we get back and I'll he able to fix ya up outa that.'[45] For those resorting to less formal arrangements, the itinerant moneylender was commonly known as the JEWMAN:

> 'What's this?' asked Father ... 'A love letter — or another solic-
> itor's letter from some curse-of-God Jewman?'
> 'It's from Lil,' said Mother.
> 'THE DEAD AROSE AND APPEARED TO MANY!' said Father. 'Take it
> away.'[46]

'The room at the front of the house was very seldom used,' Roddy Doyle remembered of his childhood: '... some people called this room the parlour and others even called it the JEWMAN'S ROOM ... if the moneylender came looking for his money he was brought in here.'[47] Front doors were left open, security devices came on four paws, and there was always a haven of sorts UP IN NELLIE'S ROOM BEHIND THE WALLPAPER.

GRAVEN IMAGES

Currency notes, apart from the universal *quid, fiver, tenner* and so on, attracted local nicknames through successive changes in design. Thus the £5 note of the 1976–90 period, featuring Catherine McAuley, was known as THE NUN WITH A PRICE ON HER HEAD, from the position of the symbol; the £10, carrying a portrait of the author, was a JOYCE. When the latter was introduced in January 1993, *The Irish Times* came up with the headline — by Joe Culley and Donal Dorcey: 'Portrait of the artist as a young tenner of note'. The thirteenth-century schoolman figuring on another £5 issue became DUNS STOCIOUS (the latter term being one of many applied to an advanced state of intoxication: see below). On the southside in particular, the £5, £10 and £20 notes were known as BUNNIES (NUNNY BUNNIES), JOYCES and DANNIES (or DANNY BOY — from the image of Daniel O'Connell) respectively. The prospect of the advent of the euro in 2002 prompted a renewed interest in the currency, as one Dublin schoolteacher discovered:

> 'How will we ask to spend a penny, Sir, after the change-over to the euro?'
> Before Bill could say 'enough of that now' a chorus rang out: 'We'll ask to leave the room to euronate'.[48]

QUID PRO QUO

The changeover meant the sudden emergence of pecuniary resources hitherto hidden from the enquiring eyes of the Revenue Commissioners: 'once the so-called MATTRESS MONEY —

undeclared income that is being spent before the currency becomes useless — is gone there may be an untimely consumer slowdown'.[49] There was also the opportunity for a fresh linguistic start, particularly as Ireland remains the only English-speaking country to embrace the currency, but it would appear to be hesitant, to say the least (as the woman said, 'why can't they wait till the old people die before they bring it in?'). 'I do miss the QUID,' Margaret Moore lamented:

> That wonderful pet name for the punt in our pockets has gone without any fanfare. The 'quid' was the true common currency. So rather than waste another minute coming up with witty names for the Millennium Spire, we should focus our energies on finding a suitable nickname for the euro.[50]

If the insistence by Brussels on the singular when referring to the currency (two euro, etc.) presented no difficulty to Hiberno-English speakers in the habit of saying 'two pound', 'thirteen pound', and so on, there was little evidence of a new vernacular emerging: YO-YO for the new unit does not seem to be achieving wide acceptance, though it is early days yet. In the meantime, the re-applied *quid* and even *pound* linger on. On the other hand, a passenger on the Ballyfermot bus was privy to the following:

> How's it going there, Patsy? Keeping well?
> SOUND AS A EURO, sound as a Euro![51]

HANG IN THERE

For many, the disbursement of money was, and is, all about, in the poet Louis MacNeice's phrase, 'The perennial if unimportant problem/Of getting enough to eat'.[52] There were, and are, many LIVING ON THE SKIN OF A RASHER or BREAD AND SCRAPE, or having to be content with a WRAP-UP, a parcel of scraps from the butcher; others, particularly the sons of doting mothers, might have been described as STALL-FED. But branded or unbranded food — and, of course, drink — had acquired a distinctively Dublin flavour long before the city woke up to the world of panini and latte and tiramisu and whatever you're having yourself. In the early years of the nineteenth century, Jonah Barrington, commenting on Donnybrook Fair, observed that 'the best tents that supplied "neat victuals" had a pot boiling outside on a turf fire, with good fat lumps of salt beef and cabbage, called SPOOLEENS, always ready simmering ...'[53] There were imports around, of course, before the recent wave of invasions: the CHIPPER was probably Italian in origin and its principal offering most certainly was, as far as the popular name was concerned. Giuseppe Cervi, according to Vincent Caprani,[54] arrived in Dublin in 1880 and began to sell chipped potatoes from a coal-fired push-cart. He prospered sufficiently to rent a premises in Great Brunswick (now Pearse) Street where his wife joined him from his native Italy. 'Signora Cervi, with very little English at her command, helped behind the counter and generally processed the take-away orders by pointing at the selection of fried fish — *uno di questo, uno di quello* [one of this and one of that]. This was soon shortened to *uno e uno*, then ONE-AND-A ONE ...':

> As down my Anna Liffey
> My love and I did stray,
> Where in the good old Liffey mud
> The seagulls sport and play
> We caught the whiff of ray and chips
> And Mary softly sighed,
> Oh! John come on for a WAN AN' WAN,
> Down by the Liffey's side.[55]

Chips, on their own, are a SINGLE. Three-quarters of a century later, in 1954, Dubliner 'Spud' Murphy marketed his Tayto crisps. The cheese and onion flavour caught on, and crisps (CRIPS) became TAYTOS thereafter. As Rosita Boland remembered: 'I thought that the brand-name Tayto was actually the word for crisps themselves.'[56] Potatoes in their unchipped state were/are known as POPPIES by the younger generation.

MARGINAL EXISTENCE

Other staples assumed their own urban identity. Pub SANGERS or SAMBOS were, before 'pub food', invariably the only solid sustenance on offer and were composed of SLICED PAN ('the greatest thing since sliced pan') smeared with MAGGY RYAN (margarine) and filled, if that is not too enthusiastic a term, with a modicum of HANG. The composition was generally known as a HANG SANG-WICH. Éamonn MacThomáis, on his city laundry rounds, missed out on the meat: 'We had our lunch on the footpath of Dunluce Road – a billycan of tea, and ten cuts of bread and Maggy Ryan.'[57] The crust of bread was the HEEL, or CATSKIN, a term also applied to the shiny crust of newly baked bread. A slice of bread was a CUT: '... he had eaten his two cuts of bread, that the shop called lunch, sitting on the step of one of the pedestals of the General Post Office ...'[58] Thick slices were DOORSTEPS. BURGOO was porridge. Sausages were SAUSINGERS: '"Haffner's pork sausingers" the Polar Bear [a nickname] narrowed down the field of research "are prime, but their birds are dear."'[59] Sausages were also, less decorously, WIDOWS' MEMORIES.

ALL WE LIKE SHEEP. . .

A BLOWOUT was a cream cake: '"What kept yis?" he roared and then he spotted the remains of the blowouts on my lips'.[60] GUR CAKE was described by Theodora Fitzgibbon as being 'eaten by the poor of Dublin in the nineteenth and early twentieth centuries, for it was very cheap, made by bakers from their stale cake or bread stocks'.[61] It was favoured by those MITCHING from school as a portable iron ration, hence to be ON THE GUR, or absent from lessons without leave. JUBILEE MUTTON, now long forgotten, dated to 1897 when Queen Victoria magnanimously distributed very small quantities of the meat to the deserving and undeserving Dublin poor, who no doubt consumed it without further adornment. The meat, however, has failed to shed its downmarket image. MUTTON DRESSED AS LAMB is still a common term of disparagement:

> As a nation, sexual liberation is really not our forte. A club near Leeson Street is dubbed GRAB A GRANNY NIGHT. One bloke asserts: 'forty-year-old women prowl the club looking for younger men, they look like mutton dressed as lamb'.[62]

And, by extension: 'when no one is looking she does try on the odd thing from Sally's wardrobe. And actually she finds those spangly platform trainers very comfortable, and not in the least MUTTONY'.[63]

Returning to our edible muttons, on a more sophisticated level, DUBLIN ROCK, again according to Theodora, was 'a rich and decorative pudding of the last century ... often decorated with angelica, blanched split almonds and branches of maidenhair fern or other plants, to look like plants growing out of a rocky hillside'.[64] (To BREAK A PUDDING, however, is to emit a loud belch.) Somewhat more evasively gastronomic is the dish alluded to by Hugh Leonard, complaining of a rival critic's view of *The Story of San Michele,* '... this is the kind of storytelling that is diminished by neither time nor fashion. Unreadable? Bernard Levin has his HASH AND PARSLEY'.[65]

BAINNE AR DHÍOL

Loose milk, delivered door to door by the milkman, whose horse responded, if reluctantly, to the command HIKE!, was poured into a can with the addition of a modicum known as a TILLY (< Irish *tuilleadh*, addition, increase), a term also used for the measure itself. The kettle would be boiling ready to refill the TIDDRER, or teapot, and WET THE TEA, preparatory to pouring: 'John came slouching down from his forge for a cup of SCALD'.[66] Those present with a half-filled cup in their hands would be offered a HOT DROP. During the Emergency (1939–45), even the simplest staples, tea especially, were in short supply, and the means to cook them equally so. This was the era of the GLIMMER-MAN (and, rarely, woman) who called at the most inopportune moments to lay his hands upon your culinary appliance to ascertain whether or not you had been using gas outside the permitted hours. A contemporary cartoon in *Dublin Opinion* depicted two upper-middle-class ladies reclining in a cell in the JOY. One says to the other: 'Well, Mrs. Fetherstonehaugh, if we have been jailed for GLIMMER-ING, what with scarcities, prices, coupons, shop assistants and all the rest of it, I'll say it's the first bit of peace we've had since the War began.' No wonder NOW YOU'RE COOKING WITH GAS! Became a synonym for conspicuous success.

BOTTOM LINE

If conspicuous excess characterises the diet of a high proportion of today's Dubs, hunger, if not an actuality, remains a potent memory reflected in such usages (note the city/culchie divide) as I COULD EAT A FARMER'S ARSE. There are many variations, extensions and modifications: the nourishing buttocks may be partaken of THROUGH A BLACKTHORN BUSH or THOUGH A HEDGE, whilst the owner thereof may be a nun or a baby, the latter featuring in the very Dublin version I COULD EAT A BABY'S BOTTOM THROUGH THE MONKEY CAGE AT THE AZOO ... hunger is its own sauce. If such meals remain conjectural, before the era of TV snacking, breakfast, dinner and tea were immovable feasts involving dietary conventions, some of which endure (TEATIME, for example, continues to be observed in news bulletins and elsewhere, even though many city workers now eat their main meal, aka dinner, in the evening). As Tom Corkery observed of the midday version of that meal, partaken of by a typical SEÁN CITIZEN of a quarter of a century ago: 'Before he may anticipate, much less partake of, his Sunday JOE SKINNER, there is a certain formality to be observed.'[67]

CAUGHT ON THE HOP

Rhyming slang, as employed here, is an importation from London cockney speech, but it has in many instances been given its own local twist. The usage is predominantly urban, as Ross O'Carroll Kelly testifies:

> I was up out of bed before 11 o'clock and — believe it or not — I was straight on the WOLFE [< Wolfe Tone: phone] trying to get myself a job . . . hit the road straightaway in order to be back in the MARGARET [< Thatcher: SCRATCHER, or bed] to see the lovely Libby with the humungous thrups on the lunchtime episode of *Neighbours.*[68]

MARGARET is interesting in employing a foreign reference for a very Dublin usage, said to date from a scabies epidemic in the city in the 1940s. Alternatively the bed in question might have been simply infested with HOPPERS:

> The Sergeant asked the justice to hear a warder as to defendant's condition. In the course of his evidence, the warder said: 'This man is infested be hoppers.'
> Justice: *Hoppers?* What is a hopper?[69]

Rhyming slang is experiencing somewhat of a revival, and most of these examples bear the stamp of indigenous authenticity; IRISH STEW and MOLLY MALONE are more probably extra-territorial:

ALLIED IRISH	< Allied Irish Bank: wank
BRENDAN GRACE	< eponymous entertainer: face
CREAM CRACKER	< knacker — member of the Travelling community
IRISH STEW:	true
JIMMY JOYCE:	voice
JOHN B:	< John B. Keane, Kerry playwright: keen
LIFFEY WATER:	porter
MOLLY MALONE:	phone
PADRAIG PEARSE	< 1916 leader: fierce (as intensifier, approx. Hiberno-English equivalent of 'very')
PEGGY DELL:	< the popular entertainer: smell.
UP THE DAMIEN:	(*cf.* Brit. slang *up the duff*, pregnant) < Damien Duff, Dublin soccer player: 'I am wearing a tracksuit bottoms masquerading as trousers and a top that sports a smock-like frontal area. Pregnant Colleague (PC) informs me these would do quite nicely should I get myself up the Damien.'[70] An alternative is UP THE BALLYJAMES < Ballyjamesduff, County Cavan.

YOUR DINNER'S POURED OUT!

In 1930, Arthur Guinness, Son & Co. (Dublin) Ltd employed upwards of 13,900 men, representing some 10 per cent of the Dublin male workforce — and a less spectacular number of women. For 277 years, UNCLE ARTHUR, his heirs and successors, were a dominant presence in Dublin life, in the areas both of production and consumption. Guinness was exported worldwide, in bottle, barrel and ultimately ships' tanks. Barrels returning to the

Dublin quays, theoretically empty, attracted the attention of PEAKERS, so called because the peaks of their caps were stained from lapping up the residue.[71] Over the course of time, the company established foreign breweries in places as far apart as London, Lagos and Kuala Lumpur, but the PRODUCT, as it was known in brewery circles, was regarded by Dubliners as something very much their own. For the summer 1969 issue of *The Harp*, the St James' Gate house journal, the then curator of the Brewery Museum, H.S. Corran, contributed an article entitled 'Ghenghis is ghoon for you. A James's gape at Guinness extracted from the usylessly unreadable Blue Book of Eccles and the proteiform graph itself':

> Give it a name, citizen, says Joe.
> Wine of the country, says he.
> What's yours? says Joe.
> DITTO MACANASPEY, says I.
> Three pints, Terry, says Joe.[72]

Corran's investigations highlighted the fact that the Joycean canon acknowledged the presence in and influence upon Dublin daily life and speech not only of Guinness but also its rivals, and which, at the time, 1904, were many: 'no matter whether it was chateaubottled Guinness's or Phoenix brewery stout it was or John Jameson and Sons or Roob Coccola or, from the matter of that, O'Connell's famous old Dublin ale that he wanted like hell ...'[73] But it was Guinness, undoubtedly, that held pride of place in the affections of the drinking classes, so much so that until relatively recently a request for 'a pint' in a Dublin pub could mean only the one thing; and it is still possible to observe, if now on rare occasions, the wordless ordering of same by a gesture involving the placing of one hand above the other, palms downward and separated by the approximate altitude of a pint glass.

PLAIN WRONG

'Do you known what I am going to tell you ... a pint of plain is your only man,' wrote Flann O'Brien,[74] and the phrase has since been deployed in many contexts both parallel and divergent, as 'Forget pints ... a glass of red is your only man'.[75] A greater sacrilege is the application of the term PLAIN to the currently available brew, it originally deriving from PLAIN PORTER, the weakest of an ascending scale that went though XX Stout to Export to FES or Foreign Extra, the latter a lethal potation best consumed, as it was intended to be, in the hidden corner of some far foreign field. Plain, as the everyday choice, carried its own abbreviation: '"Here, Pat, give us a GP, like a good fellow". The CURATE brought him a glass of plain porter.'[76] (Curates are, or were, assistant barmen.) Before the demise of plain, some connoisseurs opted for a blend of the two strengths (it was also cheaper). Samuel Beckett wrote of his character Belacqua as feeling himself 'enflamed as the Cherubim and Seraphim for all the world as though his mouth had been tapping the bung of the heavenly pipe of the fountain of sweetness instead of just coming from clipping the rim of a pint pot of HALF-AND-HALF.'[77]

The water which constituted the main ingredient of the entire range was known as LIQUOR or, with a tincture of irony as to its origins, LIFFEY WATER — THE BLACK STUFF is a more recent attribution. The QUIET PINT is a phenomenon that would seem largely to have survived the onset of musak, but once translated into the plural a FEW SCOOPS may lead more or less painlessly to a RAKE OF PINTS or, taking into account the calorific value, a meal in themselves: 'And when their grants came in and they felt like a stroll, they'd all trek up to Ranelagh for a FEED OF PINTS in the pub ...'[78] These, or their equivalent, a SLEW OF PINTS, might be consumed in the conventional manner or, alternatively: '"Yeah, yeah, yeah, we went ON THE BATTER last night. SKULLED about ten pints. Great craic."'[79]

CLERICAL ERROR

Pulling a pint was, before the advent of the IRON LUNG, a meticulous and meditative matter. But, according to Roddy Doyle, 'the drinking fraternity discovered there was a consistency to the drink from the new metal barrel, so they'd say they wanted a pint FROM THE LUNG'.[80] Patrons, however, remained watchful: a PARISH PRIEST or ROMAN COLLAR (an excessively generous head) implied short measure, quite apart from any aesthetic consideration. In the matter of consumption, due formalities were observed, particularly the ritual of buying rounds. Thus Oliver St John Gogarty:

> He smiled as we crossed Duke Street together and went upstairs to our Parnassus in the Bailey.
>
> George had come from the Brewery. Neil was there and, for a marvel, James Stephens. Neil was IN POSSESSION so Lewis took the orders.[81]

Not all imbibers, of course, were pint men (some, more cautious, would restrict themselves to a GLASHEEN — a half-pint or half, though the term is never employed); but the virtual eclipse in recent times of the bottle of stout, as opposed to the draught pint, marked another significant alteration in Dubliners' drinking habits. Pubs bottled their own, their Guinness labels proclaiming them as selling 'no other stout in bottle'. The less reputable publican was suspected of bottling re-circulated slops, known as OLD MAN. Bottles consumed, whatever the provenance of the content, were life-expired. Thus Dermot Bolger: 'A wet Saint Stephen's Day with turkey sandwiches and rows of emptied stout bottles or DEAD MEN as he called them'.[82]

WITH AN E

Some elect for the HARD STUFF, of which a ROZENER/ROSINER is a generous measure (from the rosin employed to lubricate a fiddler's bow, it was originally offered to musicians playing for dancers); a SMAHAN (< Irish *smeathán*) somewhat less generous. Of the Dublin whiskeys — Dublin, alas, no longer — Jameson was simply JJ, now perhaps more commonly JEMMY; a small bottle is a LITTLE GREEN MAN whilst its rival was, and is, a BABY POWER, the introduction of which by the distiller Sir John Power required special legislation. (Led by the ennobled Guinnesses, he and other elevated brewers and distillers were popularly known as THE BEERAGE.) 'Traditionally Dublin whiskeys were considered superior to the provincial Irish ones,' suggested John Clement Ryan, 'and to distinguish themselves the great Dublin houses always spelt their product WHISKEY and discouraged the provincial Irish houses from using this form ...'[83] A measure of an undifferentiated brand, from whatever source, is simply a BALL OF MALT. Irish coffee was a Shannon, rather than a Dublin, creation, but what about a GLORIA? 'Ruby rose and took a gulp of coffee to make room. "I'll have a gloria", she said. Reader, a gloria is a coffee laced with brany'.[84] BISHOP, or *scailtín fíona,* was a version of mulled wine involving cloves stuck into oranges and allegedly a favourite of Jonathan Swift. The Dean, according to Theodora Fitzgibbon, also had a soft spot for DUBLIN CODDLE — 'combining two of the earliest Irish foods, this has been a favourite dish since the eighteenth century'.[85] Among the plethora of contemporary potations and their defining brand-names there is still, apparently, some room for invention. Kate Holmquist wrote:

> Tomorrow, when the Junior Cert results are issued, we're likely to see such scenes as some teens spike two-litre orange bottles with litres of vodka or make DOLLY MIXTURES — soft drinks bottles filled with mixtures of whiskey, gin, vodka, beer ...[86]

PUBLIN

Drink, in its generalised, unbranded concept, is GARGLE (also a verb), or, of course, JAR, rare deficiencies of which provoke the deprived to complain that through the course of the evening nobody asked them had they a MOUTH ON THEM, while the possible cause, a pub companion reluctant to buy his round, is stigmatised as being SLOW ON THE DRAW. Dublin pubs had, until the recent appearance of the super-pub, remained little changed over the past 200 years. Fergus Linehan lamented:

> The death of Maureen Potter breaks a link that goes back almost two centuries to the old FREE AND EASIES, the singing and performing pubs of the eighteenth and early nineteenth centuries.[87]

'... in Dublin city,' according to Tom Corkery, '... a pub is either a SINGING-HOUSE with a special lounge entirely given over to music, or else a strict non-singing house where the first threat of the note being held aloft will send the landlord rushing headlong for the Law.'[88] Not falling within this distinction was the MARKET HOUSE, a pub permitted by law to open at crack of dawn to serve the needs of market workers, dockers and the temporarily or permanently unemployed in dire need of a cure. The old order changes, of course: According to Sorcha Griffith, 'Ringsend is dotted with pubs that some young people refer to as OLD-MAN PUBS, but they are a dying breed.'[89]

NOW, GENTLEMEN, PLEASE

The Law enshrined the niceties of the labyrinth of licensing regulations, amongst which were a period of closure, instituted by the first Minister for Justice, Kevin O'Higgins, known as the HOLY HOUR or simply HH, from 14.30 to 15.30 on weekdays, designed, so was theory, to allow the habitual drinker home for his dinner. Sean King, a barman in the Bailey, told Ulick O'Connor:

I left a young waiter in charge of the bar for the last five minutes before closing time. The lad had no experience of this sort of thing. I warned him not to serve anyone, even if it was the President, once the Holy Hour had begun ... A few minutes later there was a shocking row in the bar. I rushed in. A portly gentleman was roaring — 'Do you think I am a bloody chronometer? I asked your man for a drink and he asks me the time'. This was Brendan Behan.[90]

On Sundays, matters were worse, from the dedicated drinker's point of view: the hour-long FIRST SESSION from 13.30 — later 12.30 — was succeeded by a long DROUTH until the opening of the SECOND SESSION at 17.00. When last drinks were called and the then-notional drinking-up time generally long expired, the familiar mantra was uttered: 'Now, gents, please, it's gone the time ... have ye no homes to go to?' and in spite of the many relaxations in licensing hours, that dismissive phrase still lives. At the time of the debate in 2005 over the possibility of introducing more civilised drinking in establishments on the continental model, a newspaper cartoon depicted the then Minister for Justice and Bar Reform in his role as a publican addressing two un-co-operative patrons: 'Have yez no café bars to go to?'

TRAVELLERS' TALES

When time had been called, a predictable request was for just one more round — expressed as A BANG OF THE LATCH. On receiving the half-expected refusal, a drinker had no alternative but the BONAFIDE. DOING THE BONAFIDE or GOING ON THE BONES involved travelling to a pub a minimum of three miles beyond the city limits. Introduced for legitimate travellers under the Licensing Act of 1874, and abolished as late as 1960, the procedure invited a range of abuses, both legal and alcoholic, all of which were ignored or derided by those BLUE MOULDY or GUMMING FOR A PINT after normal hours. And since bona-fide status was based on your home address, many thus ineligible southsiders (Matt Smith's in Stepaside, south County Dublin, was a popular resort) became northsiders for the night, FOUND-ONS (those found illegally on the premises) offering raiding gardaí addresses in suburbs they would normally not acknowledge as within the embrace of civilisation. At times, discovery by the Law was averted by barring the doors, dousing the lights and confining those on the premises to an unlit inner room. 'Adulthood arrived with the sweet taste of forbidden fruit,' confessed Fergus Cassidy, 'the pub LOCK-IN.'[91]

UP IN SMOKE

The American humorist, Art Buchwald, experienced the Dublin bona-fide system at the time in the 1950s when John A. O'Brien's book *The Vanishing Irish*, highlighting the emigration drain, was attracting unfavourable local attention. His reaction, according to Myles na gCopaleen, was: 'The Irish are not vanishing. They are just moving rapidly from place to place to get drinks after hours.' But all that is long gone. Now, the focus is on the nicotine addicts, legally expelled from their alcoholic Arcadia and obliged to stand outside the pub in the rain to satisfy the craving. When the Act was due to come into force in 2004, 'what Moriarty is least looking forward to is the influx of what he calls NOODIE NAADIES in his bar,' reported Roisín Ingle: 'Noodie Naadies are nosy people who haven't been to a pub in years and will just come in from Monday to see whether people are smoking.'[92] 'This legislation has created a new social activity: SMIRTING,' concluded Ross Golden-Bannon: 'Flirting and smoking is all the rage and non-smokers often head to the outdoor smoking area for the banter.'[93]

CRÚISCÍN LÁN

All good innocent fun; but the consequences of A FEW SCOOPS, or LIFTING THE LITTLE FINGER too much,[94] if not perhaps measurable in terms of today's binge-drinking, as often as not resulted in a condition variously described as BALUBAS, BLADDERED, BOLLOXED, BULLAPHANTS — to cite only a few examples under the letter B. 'The fact is, that there's a pretty thick line between having A FEW JARS and enjoying yourself, and getting bladdered', claimed Paddy Murray,[95] but be that as it may, the euphemisms employed to denote the condition testify as to its core role in the social environment. The Spanish lexicographer, José Manuel Lechado García, in his dictionary of euphemisms,[96] lists only nine relating to intoxication as against 72 for *follar* ('fuck', the verb). What this reveals about the relative predilections of Dubliners and Madrileños is open to debate, but it can be said with small fear of contradiction that the terms employed by the former in respect of the state of having DRINK TAKEN are not only more numerous but considerably more colourful and inventive. Not all, of course, could be defined as purely or even predominantly Dublin; but a relevant short list might include:

BALUBAS Came into the lexicon as a term of generalised contempt in the 1960s following the disastrous encounter between a Belgian Congo tribe of that name and the Irish forces serving with the UN. Presumed extinct, it has how arisen and appeared to many as an adjective, describing an advanced state of intoxication: 'Less dancing at the crossroads than balubas on drink at the crossroads.'[97]

FLUTHERED; FLUTHERY-EYED 'a man seen more than the queen of

France and him out in a boat fishin', coopers of stout and sandwiches, half-fallin' out of the boat rotten fluthery-eyed drunk . . . .'[98]

FOOTLESS

GARGLED

GEE–EYED   < GEE, vagina.

IN THE JIGS

JARRED   — most usually '... out of one's mind'.

HORRENDIFIED   'In the RDS, roysh, and me and the goys had made plans to get totally horrendified ...'[99]

MAGGOTY

MAGGOTY MOULDY

MAITHGOLORS   < Irish *maith go leor*, good enough, all right.

MOULDY

MULLERED   'I follow him down to the study, where of course Hennessy's mullered as well.'[100]

NOURISHED

OSSIFIED   Word-play on 'stoned'.

PARLATIC   < *paralytic*, by omission and transposition. '"The majority up there", he said, "is young blades getting parlatic on the smell of a cork ..."'[101]

PELOOTHERED   < POLLUTED + FLUTHERED.

PETRIFIED   See OSSIFIED.

POLLUTED

RAT-ARSED   'The whole enjoyment and business of life of the "bucks" seemed to consist of eccentricity and violence ... one can only conclude that they were rat-arsed with drink ...'[102]

RAT–FACED	'We had a wonderful time doing it [*Hall's Pictorial Weekly*, TV series] remembers [Frank] Kelly. "Then we'd all go to Madigan's and get RAT FACED."'[103]
ROTTO	
SCUTTERED	< SCUTTER, excrement < Irish *sciodar*, diarrhoea.
SKANKY.	Originally US slang: 'dirty, second-rate, unattractive, cheap-looking, ugly' or the reverse, 'attractive, sexy' (of a woman).[104]
TRANSMOGRIFIED	
TROLLEYED	
TROUSERED	
WASTED	Shay was sitting at the table, wasted from the bottle of whiskey Justin had purchased.'[105]

... to take only a quick run at the alphabet.

BUNNY FARM

All of which goes to show that 'Drink', as John Waters views it, 'is an inseparable element of social life in Ireland. Indeed you might unexceptionably write the last sentence without the world "social" in it.'[106] As for those, he said, who do not, 'as we delicately tend to put it, TAKE A DRINK ... you become an object of suspicion when you either stop going into pubs or, having once "taken a drink" continue to go into pubs while declining what will often on such occasions be accusingly referred to as a REAL DRINK.' And as for confronting the after-effects of the latter: for the inescapably CRAW-SICK, the only remedy is:

THE CURE. A word in frequent use in Dublin. It is the drink taken in the morning to recover from the effects of a hard night ... An alternative phrase is A HAIR OF THE DOG THAT BIT YOU, which [Oliver St John] Gogarty suggested may also be used to explain why women in childbirth prefer men to women doctors.[107]

There are other remedies. Writing of a family furry friend, Fiona Looney admitted:

The rabbit has just spent a week in the Priory. I always knew some member of our family would, but to be honest, I always thought the safe money was on me. Still, when The Priory in question is not the celebrity WRINGER-OUTER but a boarding kennel, I suppose I should be grateful to be overlooked.[108]

We had better leave it at that.

6

LAMENT FOR
MOUSEY RYAN

'Peg' Woffington ... made her first appearance on the regular
stage in the part of 'Ophelia' at the Aungier Street house; but
deserted it in 1742 for Smock Alley, where she appeared on
15th June as 'Sir Harry Wildair', her favourite part, varying her
performance however by playing 'Ophelia' to Garrick's
'Hamlet'. So crowded were the houses during this engagement,
that a pestilential epidemic ensued, playfully known in Dublin
as the GARRICK FEVER.

> Samuel A. Ossory Fitzpatrick, *Dublin, A Historical and
> Topographical Account of the City* (1907).

Samuel Lewis published his two-volume *Topographical
Dictionary of Ireland* in 1837 to general acclaim. In the
course of his detailed survey of Dublin, he concluded that

The places of public amusement are few. The drama is little
encouraged by the fashionable and wealthy; the theatre is thinly
attended, except on the appearance of some first-rate performer
from London, or at the special desire of the lord lieutenant, the
social character of the inhabitants inducing an almost exclusive
preference to convivial intercourse within the domestic circle.

In the same paragraph, however, he appears to contradict himself by informing the reader of the New Theatre Royal in Hawkins Street, 'a pile of unsightly exterior but internally of elegant proportions', which had opened its doors in 1821, as well as another theatre, opened in February of the year of the publi-cation of his *Dictionary*, under the title of 'Theatre Royal, Irish Opera House, Lower Abbey-street, under the King's Patent, granted to Messrs. Jones, of the original Theatre Royal, Crow-street'.[1] He also lists 'another small theatre in Fishamble-street, called the Adelphi', as well as 'the Rotundo gardens' (which were subsequently to undergo a sex-change to ROTUNDA), the scene of 'occasional exhibitions of rope-dancing and fireworks'.

GIVING A HOOT

Over the course of much of the previous century, the Dublin the-atres had seen fireworks in plenty — more than one theatre being burned to the ground through the actions of a disrespect-ful audience. The theatre offered Dubliners the opportunity of exercising their wit and malice both on and off the stage, a trait reflected in their ingrained predilection for applying nicknames to all and sundry. Anne Catley, a celebrated singer, affected a hair-style that became the Dublin fashion and was known as CATLEYFIED HAIR. The former actor, Henry Mossop, a Dubliner who succeeded Thomas Sheridan as manager of the Smock Alley Theatre, was known as the TEAPOT ACTOR 'on account of his favourite attitude — one hand on hip, the other stretched upward'.[2] George Faulkner, the prominent printer who took himself very seriously, was ridiculed by the playwright and actor, Samuel Foote, as PETER PARAGRAPH: 'Faulkner sent his employees to hoot the actor from the stage, but the comedian took him off so well that everyone stayed to enjoy the fun ...'[3] In the Theatre Royal on 17 June 1828,

Mr Luke Plunkett made his first appearance as "Richard III". Mr Plunkett was a most respectable and intelligent gentleman, only eccentric on one point — he thought himself the greatest Richard III in existence; he was in consequence called MAD PLUNKETT.[4]

Ten years later, in the same theatre, the Dublin Militia, who were called in to provide — to disastrous effect — the echoes in a performance of *Der Freischutz*, were known as the DIRTY DUBS (the abbreviation has a long and variegated history).

ACTS OF THE GODS

There were nicknames, too, for the theatre itself. 'The upper boxes, in a line with the two-shilling gallery, were called LATTICES, and over them, even with the shilling gallery, were the SLIPS, also termed PIGEON-HOLES.[5] The upper gallery, or 'the gods', was habitually the source of repartee between actor and audience. In 1776, an actor by the name of John Henry Johnston was playing in *Much Ado About Nothing* at the Crow Street Theatre. He had borrowed the sum of 10s 1d from one Jemmy, proprietor of a tennis court in Dame Street, which he had failed to repay. He was interrupted in his rendering of 'Sigh no more, Ladies' by a chanting from the gallery: 'Jacky Johnston, Jacky Johnston, Oh you owe me, you owe me, you owe me, ten and a penny'. The defaulter paid up then and there.[6] In January 1821, the year the Royal in Hawkins Street first opened its doors, Pat M'Keon, a painter turned actor and singer, was a popular success.

A very favourite song of M'Keon was an old ballad called 'Your Melting Sighs reach my Heart'. On one occasion, when he arrived at the words, 'Your melting sighs', one of his friends in the upper gallery called out, 'Ah! Now, Pat, sure you had enough of MELTIN' SIZE when you were a painter.'[7]

In 1850, another actor, a Mr Hudson, found himself very much under the shadow of the great Tyrone Power. When he attempted a performance of a song in which the latter excelled, a voice from the Theatre Royal gallery called out 'very fair, Hudson, and MORE POWER to you'. In recent times, the original building which housed the National Theatre, formerly the city morgue, was known as the OUL' SHABBEY. When the Gate Theatre set up in rivalry, producing at the time morally suspect drama in contrast to the kitchen come-dies served up at the older institution, the two were popularly known as SODOM AND BEGORRAH, a reference to the sexual propensi-ties of the Gate's founding directors. Whatever about the impre-sarios, Dublin theatre audiences, however, are apparently nowadays somewhat more deferential. 'First night is invite night,' advises Belinda McKeon, 'so yes, that probably is Gay Byrne over there. If you must GAWK, get it over with before the show begins.'[8]

GAME OF THE NAME

'Nicknames were among the many things that enriched my youth,' confessed Vincent Caprani,

> . . . my neighbourhood in Dublin and my apprenticeship to the printing trade. In those days — the 1940s and '50s — almost everyone possessed a nickname, complimentary or otherwise. They were lavished on the high-born and the low, on priest, politician and poltroon, and they were broadcast frequently with mischievous — and occasionally with malicious! — intent ... The apposite nickname became a sort of shorthand to label everything from a person's physical prowess, physical features or physical defects to a pithy description of his trade or calling, his social, political or religious background. It became a life-long tag which helped to deflate the pompous, or to elevate the nonentity to something akin to immortality. In practically all cases the nickname usurped the baptismal name ...[9]

C.S. Andrews suffered the same experience:

> A curious feature of my Terenure life was the fact that nearly all the boys and many of the men had nicknames — Tipp Dwyer, Nauch McGrath, Giller Guilfoyle, Monkey Donovan — and in due course I acquired my own nickname, Todd ... 'Todd' stuck to me so firmly that it became my Christian name, even amongst my own family ...[10]

CLASS DISTINCTIONS

The practice began early. Paddy Crosbie recalled the 'amazing collection of nicknames' among his classmates at the Christian Brothers', North Brunswick Street, otherwise THE BRUNNER:

> There was BOXER FOLEY, DARKIE SULLIVAN, SNOWBALL BALFE, HARRIER DEVINE, MUTTONER DUNN, HOBBY DUNN, WHACKER MOORE, WHACKER DOWDALL, GERO, MOUSEY RYAN, SONDSER QUINN, the two HARROS, GIANT BRENNAN, CHICKEN BYRNE, GLAXO GORMAN, SNUB BOLLARD, MUCKY MAHER ... YEEMO GAFFEY, DOUGH CALLAN, LEADNER MURPHY, MARY O'BRIEN, PARKY RYAN, STEVE DONOGHUE, TIGER LYONS, EYEBROWS O'BRIEN, PUDDENER O'BRIEN, RAMSEY MCDONNELL ... The teachers did not escape and old BRUNNERITES will remember LANNYLEGS, CHENTY, JUICY and NAPOLEON.[11]

Most Dublin schools boasted, and continue to boast, nicknames. According to Gus Smith, the TV presenter Eamonn Andrews 'was amused to find that boys in Synge Street were called CANARIES because of the pronunciation of the school name.'[12] In the eighteenth century, an English gunsmith, John Molyneux, settled in Dublin. There, he claimed, his operations ... supported twenty English families, two BLUE BOYS at the King's Hospital, apprentices and workmen.'[13] The nickname reflected the colour of the uniform.

A POLICEMAN'S LOT

Youthful nicknames generally connoted half-derisory affection rather than active malice, a quality not entirely absent from nicknaming in the adult world, though the Dubliner has always exhibited an innate ability to temper malice with wit. 'I've known cops,' wrote Éamonn MacThomáis, 'by the name of LUGS, BRASSO, RED NECK, FLAT FOOT, PORTER BELLY, TARPO, GOGO, BLUE BOTTLE and a dozen other names I could not put into print.'[14] A familiar figure in 1950s Dublin was a huge garda who used to do duty at the O'Connell Bridge end of Westmoreland Street — he was known universally and affectionately as TINY. Such affection did not always extend to the force as a whole, or to its predecessor, the DMP (Dublin Metropolitan Police):

> 'In London ... a policeman has only to put up his hand, and it is sufficient. It is not so in Dublin', complained one traffic constable. This 'contrariness' as regards traffic extended even to Dublin's upper classes for, as our constable further explained, 'if you speak to a gentleman ... many of them will tell you that you are a CAD OF A POLICEMAN or some other offensive expression.'[15]

There were other equally unflattering appellations. In the eighteenth century, according to Peter Somerville-Large, most policing was done by patrolling watchmen appointed by parish charities. 'As a result they were often old and feeble. William Le Fanu described these CHARLEYS with their lanterns, long frieze coats and capes with low-crowned hats.'[16] For Sean O'Casey and his contemporaries, the law was to be kept at a safe distance. '"The less anyone has to do with HARVEY DUFFS an' HORNEYS the better", he said: ready to swear a hole through an iron pot.'[17] Commonly at that time and after, they were also RAWSERS or RASSERS — the Dublin pronunciation of 'rozzer'. Brendan Behan added his own colour: 'He admitted that he was drunk and apologised for his language. Witnesses said that he called policemen murderers, SCRUFFHOUNDS and DIRT BIRDS.'[18]

TOUCHING SCENE

MacThomáis recalls a familiar Dublin character of the past known as the TOUCHER DOYLE, alleged to have successfully TOUCHED the visiting Prince of Wales for five shillings. He may (or may not) have inspired Myles na gCopaleen's anecdote concerning an impecunious petty princeling who was apt to bestow honours in return for unrepayable loans. As Myles described it, adapting Dr Johnson's verdict on Goldsmith: '*neminem ornavit quem non tetegit* [he adorned none whom he did not touch]'.[19] A PATENT TOUCHER 'is one more skilled than his brethren at his job ... Then there was the SEMI-TOUCHER, who used to stride through the streets with a scythe over his shoulder; he used to cut lawns and was only known to touch for tobacco.'[20] But nicknames, like so much else, would seem to have succumbed to the sterile blight of political correctness, where an inability to appreciate the finer points of quaternions can no longer be equated with 'intellectual disability' for fear of giving offence. Red Neck, Flat Foot and Porter Belly have retreated before the uninventive sobriquets of the soccer field. Politicians, once the recipients of nicknames such as BLADDER CHOPS (Lord Norbury, the hanging judge), are now let off with half-respectful sobriquets such as THE ROTTWEILER (the current [2006] PEE DEE[21] Minister for Justice). As for the incumbent Taoiseach: 'Now look here', admonishes Pat Leahy: 'It's one thing THE BERT swanking around with his fellow world leaders dressed in the canary yellow trousers and nearly matching jacket ...'[22] The model, of course, is the generally affectionate THE MAMMY/THE DA/THE BROTHER etc., reflecting the Irish-language deployment of the definite article.

HE'S BEHIND YOU!

Before foreign games in the form of British soccer came to fill every waking hour, the PICTURES had succeeded the theatre as a popular leisure choice, particularly among the young. 'Regarding the SHAKY PICTURES which we were brought to see in the Rotunda Rooms,' said Moira Lysaght, 'all that I seem to remember is that they were very shaky indeed ...'[23] C.S. Andrews recalled, 'There were occasional visits to the Rotunda or the LIVING PICTURES ... and they were really no better than animated photographs. There was no story line, just characters chasing one another.'[24] For a later generation, the PENNY RUSH, TWOPENNY RUSH, FOURPENNY RUSH or SIX-PENNY RUSH (depending upon the year and the rate of inflation) was 'the highlight of the week. Some people say that the Penny Rush was originally a South City feature in the Abercorn. I do not dispute that, but I can tell them that *the* Penny Rush took place every Saturday in the late Teens and early Twenties at the Phoenix Cinema on Ellis Quay.'[25] The kids had their own names for their favourite picture-houses, amongst which were:

BROAD	The Broadway, Manor Street
CORE	Inchicore
DORRIER	Dorset Street
ELECK	The New Electric, Talbot Street
FEENO	Phoenix Picture Palace, Ellis Quay
FIZZER	Blacquire Bridge
FOUNTAIN	James' Street
LOUSEBANK	The Lyceum, formerly the Volta, once managed, not very successfully, by James Joyce
LUX	The De Luxe, Camden Street
MAYRO	Mary Street Picture House
PRINNER	The Princess, Rathmines Road
RI	Rialto
ROTO	The Rotunda, Parnell Square
TIVO	The Tivoli, Francis Street

At one period, entry could be gained by the offer of jam jars in lieu of cash. 'That happened in the Twopenny Rush days,' Éamonn MacThomáis recalled:

> If you handed in a threepenny bit you might be stuck with two one pound jam jars for your change. Can you imagine sitting on the WOODENERS, trying to balance two jam jars, peel your orange, and keep your eye on the CHAP, the MOT and the Crook ...[26]

In terms of comfort, the CUSHIONERS were slightly superior to the woodeners, but there was generally no distinction in their price, in jam jars or otherwise. The screen hero, whether of the big picture or of the FOLLYER-UPPER or weekly serial — forerunner of the television soap— was known as the Chap, his partner in the barely-tolerated love-interest as the Mot or the girl. Too many trailers or other irrelevant matter would invoke the cry SHOW THE PICTURE! Not everyone, for financial reasons or otherwise, was able to see all the desirable pictures, so the practice prevailed of TELLING A PICTURE, one of the lucky ones recounting the action to an attentive audience of the deprived.

COME IN OURA THAT!

Otherwise, kids (and, indeed, adults) provided their own street entertainment, played out on the stone setts or DURLOGUES (< Irish *duirleog*, round stone) and much of it as formally structured as any of today's staged parades, and accompanied in many instances by verbal rituals as invariable as the rules of the game. According to Leslie Daiken:

> Dublin's treasurehouse of guff is her own very special, vintage. Rich as GUR-CAKE. Garnished with gobstopper juice: ground-up with the spice of stones found in deserted lots: kneaded-in with the messes of thick mud in laneways gas-lit, and roads

stone-set, where endless drizzly rain-rain-rain, and damp, gave to the local taste its consistency ... However transient, street rhymes and slogans give to the life of a town a stamp and a date-mark, like nothing else does.[27]

'Kids were playing under a street-lamp by the tram-stop at Sally's Bridge. "P'liceman, p'liceman, don't take me. Take that boy behind the tree. He took silver, he took gold, p'liceman, p'liceman, please take hold."'[28] There was H.O.H.A! (pronounced *Haitch Oh Haitch Ah*), 'hit one hit all', the war-cry in street gang battles; TIP 'N' TIG (or tag) rhymes and skipping rhymes and the gamut of games themselves:

BALL IN THE DECKER	Rolling a ball into caps (deckers) placed against a wall.
BILLY FOX TAIL	Leapfrog game involving two teams.
BILLY RUMP STICKS	
DAB-OUT	Game featuring a number of marbles placed in a chalked ring. Each marble knocked out by a TAW became the property of the player.
DUCK ON THE GRAWNSHEE	(< Irish *gráinseach*, granary, farm) A game with marbles.
FOLLY	Pursuit-and-strike marbles game.
HOLE 'N' TAW	Marbles game involving three holes in the ground.
HOP AND COCK-A-ROOSHY	Two-team game. 'After tossing head or harp with a penny, one team stood in the roadway, while the other stayed on the path. The object now was for the team on the path to get as many as possible across the road to the other side of the street.'[29]
JACK, JACK SHOW THE LIGHT	

KATTIE or CAT — A game played on the path-edge and the roadway with a short stick and a long one.

KICK THE CAN — 'I think this was invented for those who couldn't afford a football. The boy ON IT stood by the can, and we had to kick the can without the boy "on it" touching us.'[30]

MAKE-IN — Played with a make, or halfpenny

MOWL (< 'hole') — Game involving lifting the cover of a water hydrant and firing pennies into it.

PIGGY BEDS — Played on chalked geometrical BEDS on the pavement The PIGGY or PICKY could be an old shoe-polish tin, kicked on one foot from square to square. A narrow rectangular section of the bed was known as the SKINNY EIGHT. Another name for this game was TRANCE, also used as a verb: '"Anywhere here", said Uncle Tom suddenly ... "where we could thrance [*sic*] the youngster, an' go for a drink?"'[31]

PUSSY-FOUR-CORNERS — A kind of rounders played without a ball.

RELIEVIO — 'When darkness fell people awaited the lamplighter with his magic wand to light the glass globe so that children could play relievio or other street games ...'[32]

ROPE THE DOOR — Tying a rope to a door knob and pulling it hard against whoever tried to open it in response to a knock.

TAW IN THE HOLE   A game with marbles. MEBS were small marbles; a GULL or GULLIER was a king marble; a DAB the equivalent of the British 'taw', though that term was also heard.

THREE-AND-IN   'Now I watched the ball smash against the gate as one boy scored a goal, they were playing Three-And-In, there was no room for a fourth player even if they bothered to speak to me.'[33]

STRINGING ALONG

Less formalised games or pastimes included BOXING THE FOX: robbing an orchard; KNICK-KNOCKS: ringing a doorbell and running away, also known as THUNDER AND LIGHTNING; and, when there used to be real icy winters, HUNKER-SLIDING, which curiously became a synonym for shirking work or general duplicity. Similarly anti-social was MIND THE THREAD:

> Two boys, one at each side of the path, would sit on the ground pretending to hold a piece of thread between them ... the game would suddenly start as a man or a woman came walking up the path. As soon as they came quite near, one of the boys would start shouting 'Mrs., Mrs., mind the thread'. The poor woman thinks there's a thread on the ground so she starts lifting her legs, jumping and dancing to avoid the thread.[34]

A century earlier, anti-social behaviour was equally prevalent amongst Dublin's young. Jonah Barrington confessed, 'We used to convey gunpowder squibs into all the lamps in several streets at once, breaking every lamp to SHIVERS.'[35] Girls played MAKEY-UP or MAKEY-UPPY games like shops, using CHAINIES — broken bits of china and delft — as IMMO (imitation) money; real shops provided such delicacies as SLIDERS — ice-cream wafers — PEGGY'S LEG, NANCY BALLS (< 'aniseed') or, available only at Christmas and Easter, HALF-TIME JIMMIES, a succulent chocolate bar. If you had the readies for these, you were unquestionably IN YOUR GRANNIE'S.

PENO, REF!

Street football after school was played with a SHAMMIER, or tennis ball, kicked along the path. Grown-up games, apart from the nicknames of teams and players, tend to lack the same degree of localised reference, and many of these, particularly regarding the participants, prove to be ephemeral. There are those, however, which have achieved a more permanent presence. A random selection across several sports would include HEFFO'S HEROES, the Dublin GAA team, captained by Kevin Heffernan, which won the 1974 football final with the support of HEFFO'S ARMY; a couple of decades later, Hill 16 at CROKER hailed another Dubs hero, Jason Sherlock:

Boom, boom, boom,
Everybody say JAYO,
Jaaayoooo!!

Meanwhile, soccer venues at home and abroad echoed to OOH-AAH PAUL MCGRATH, the fan greeting for the former star of Dalkey United. The phrase DO A RONNIE DELANY, to run in emulation of the winner of the 1,500 metres in the 1956 Olympics, also entered the lexicon. Nicknames for sporting clubs favour the simple abbreviation: THE DUBS in this context are the GAA team or teams, though 'Walsh Park was a reminder of how far THE METROPOLITANS (as papers used to call the Dubs when I was young) have still to come.'[36] Among the city soccer clubs are, or were, BOHS (Bohemians), also known a shade more imaginatively as THE

155

GYPSIES; SHELS (Shelbourne); and DRUMS (Drumcondra). Shamrock Rovers are THE HOOPS, from the strip design. Rugby and its followers considered themselves to occupy a superior level. 'Certainly, sensible people would fear excesses of George Hook-style rugger-bugger bluster,' asserted Eddie Holt. 'But allowing for such inevitable ALICK-ADOODOM and a spate of Clongowian clowning, an Irish triumph would be celebrated as a victory for Celtic passion ...'[37] That obscure abstract noun apparently derives from a book by one Alec Kadoo, said to have so occupied a team colleague whilst on a train journey that he refused to play cards with the great W.E. 'Ernie' Crawford of Lansdowne, capped 30 times for Ireland.

Of Dublin's many soccer stars, not a few received their early training on the streets.

Andy Reid breaks into a broad smile when asked to explain what LAMPER is. 'It's about where we come from,' the young Dubliner says ... Reid grew up playing 'lamper' – trying to score in impromptu, harem-scarem kickabouts using just a 'skinny' lamppost as a goal.[38]

Looking forward to the future career of Johnny Giles, Malachy Clerkin wrote: 'He's known all across the city as its best schoolboy footballer BY A STREET and within a year or so Manchester United will spirit him away.'[39] The political columnist of *The Irish Times* wrote: 'That phrase oft heard on the playing fields of Dublin, "WATCH YOUR HOUSE" is a personal motto of Drapier ...'[40] In the game of handball, a CANTED ball is one struck by mistake out of court, hence a ball in a game of street soccer sent over a wall and thus irretrievable is 'canted'. From the same sport of handball comes GAME BALL, the last round of the game, generally adopted to indicate that everything is ok, as in the Dublin street rhyme, 'How's your oul' wan? Game ball!' In a similar sense but now less common is LINE BALL, as employed by W.T. Cosgrave, President of the Executive Council, in the Dáil in 28 November

1922, speaking of the inadequacies of the Dublin & Blessington tramway: '...the line has many twists and turns which make it very expensive to run. I understand that itwould be possible line ball if it were to run from Dublin to Tallaght'.[41] (Another expression of complete satisfaction is THE JOB'S OXO, the familiar meat cube taking on the implications of 'ok': 'Marty [Minister Martin Cullen] was a great man for consultants. As long as I had the right credentials, the job was oxo'.[42])

VOX POPULI

In spite of the intrusion of the 'corporate' world, immured behind glass panels and prawn sandwiches, into the popular environs of DALYER (Dalymount Park) and other long-established sporting venues, what Tom Corkery described in 1980 as 'the authentic voice of the terraces' is still to be heard, in spite of 'that crowd in thar':

> It's a disgrace, that's wha' it is, the number a people that's been let in, it's on-huming [inhuman]. ON-HUMING; yez'd think we wus cattles or somethin'. Suppposin', I MEAN JEST SUPPPOSIN' SOMETHIN' WUS TO HAPPEN. Wha' chances has anny of us. Why, we'd be murthered ... lookit them misfawrtnit chislers over thar under the wall, I ask yez wha' chances has them misfawrtnit chislers if annythin' was to happen to that wall? But wha' do THAT CROWD IN THAR care about you or me or them misfawertnit chislers! THAT CROWD IN THAR isn't out for you or me. THAT CROWD IN THAR IS ONEY OUT FOR THEIRSELVES ...[43]

Contemporary sporting rhetoric, however, has apparently settled for the lowest common denominator, as reported by Nuala O'Faolain from CROKER:

The last line [of the National Anthem] is traditionally lost in a roar of pure excitement and the crowd melts into a mass of tribal empathy and in a hail of filthy language — of which it is completely unconscious ... shouting EFFIN BOLLIX at the ref, groaning FOR FUXXAKE at wides, issuing instructions — 'fuxxake get in front of Seán Óg!' 'C'mon Gilly, for fuxxsake'.[44]

BANGING AWAY

The eighteenth-century Dubliner, however, took his sport where he found it, and, as far as the upper levels of society were concerned, that was as likely as not on the duelling field. Jonah Barrington recalled:

About the year 1777, the FIRE-EATERS were in great repute in Ireland. No young fellow could finish his education till be had exchanged shots with some of his acquaintances. The first two questions asked as to a young man's respectability and qualifications ... were 'What family is he of?' — 'Did he ever BLAZE?'[45]

To blaze, one required BARKING-IRONS, of course, otherwise long-barrelled POINT-BLANKERS or POINT-BLANKS. The gun deployed by the supporters of Robert Emmet's 1803 rising was known affectionately as a NANCY: 'Three hours I lay bleeding/My Nancy by my side ...'[46] The BUCKS and BLOODS, amongst them those who founded the legendary HELL FIRE CLUB in the Dublin mountains, were not averse to turning their weapons on innocent strangers. Some of their number were known as SWEATERS or PINKINDINDIES.

The former practised SWEATING, that is forcing persons to deliver up their arms; the latter cut off a small portion from the ends of their scabbards, suffering the naked point to project; with these they prodded or pinked those unoffending passers-by on whom they thought fit to bestow their attentions.[47]

Even more malevolent were the upper-class hooligans nick-named CHALKERS, who attacked and seriously disabled people, apparently just for the hell of it.

GET THEE TO THE NUNNERY. . .

This was, of course, serious criminal activity by any standards, and it took place in a city that pullulated, both then and later, with crime of all degrees. Prisons, such as the Sheriff's Marshalsea, known as the BLACK DOG, were uniformly appalling.

> A report of a committee of the Irish House of Commons in 1729 described how every prisoner had to pay towards the PENNY POT — 2s 2d at the Black Dog and 1s 4d at Newgate with another 4d added for 'not being thrown into the FELON'S ROOM' ... the really destitute were imprisoned in a small, foul room known as THE NUNNERY, because women arrested by the watch were confined there together with howling and cursing male criminals.[48]

Those incarcerated, even under these conditions, might, however, have counted themselves fortunate: common penalties were hanging or transportation to Van Diemen's Land even for what would nowadays be considered minor crimes. It was a minor crime indeed, in the eighteenth-century context, that merited nothing more severe than the stocks. Gallows humour was, however, an abiding characteristic of the Dublin criminal classes: 'What Englishman would ever have thought of calling persons in the pillory THE BABES IN THE WOOD', marvelled the Edgeworths:

> This is a common cant phrase among Dublin reprobates. Undoubtedly these humorous cant phrases among profligates tend to lessen the power of shame, and the effect of punish-ment; and a witty rogue will lead numbers to the gallows.[49]

A BIT IN DEIR SACKS

Writing of Dublin slang songs of the 1780s, Donal O'Sullivan observed:

> They show the environment and outlook (slightly heightened, doubtless, for dramatic effect) of a section of the community who lived in constant dread of the gallows ... Some of the slang words occurring in these songs seem to be unrecorded and others are dated by the compilers of dictionaries as nineteenth century. Most of them seem to belong to the sort of thieves' slang which is common to both Ireland and Great Britain, except such words as SHEBEEN and CRETUR peculiar to Ireland.[50]

Typical is the popular ballad, 'De Night Before Larry was Stretch'd' (see page 72). Apart from the slang terms themselves, the orthography is a fair representation of Dublin speech, particularly 'the difficulty of pronouncing *th*', as O'Sullivan puts it, and the strong past tense RIZ for 'raised'. Similarly the opening stanza of 'Luke Caffrey's Ghost':

> Oh! De time-piece had come to de twelves,
> De FARDINS burn'd blue in deir sockets, [< 'farthing dip', a cheap candle]
> When REE RAW and I be ourselves [nickname of an elusive footpad, < Irish *rí-rá*, hubbub or uproar]
> De bottle took out of our pockets;
> De stiff was betuxt where we sat, ['betwixt']
> As blind as de box of a pedlar;
> We drank to his helt for all that,
> While we curst de neck-hampring medler.
> *(to be spoken):* dat stud upon de green clot, badgered poor Luke's STAGS [professional bailsman or alibi-provider] out of court and took away his precious life for de valiatin of a few

hump-back'd WILLIAMITES [?William III copper halfpenny] and a bloody Queen Anne's TESTER [sixpence], your soul.'

GAOLWORDS

'Luke Caffrey's Kilmainham Minit' [MINIT was the Dublin pronunciation of 'minuet', the macabre dance at the end of a rope] reflected the fact that 'the most extreme form of punishment was execution. Taking place mainly at the HANGING TREE in St Stephen's Green, outside Newgate Prison, at GALLOWS HILL in Kilmainham and on Kilmainham Common, executions were manifestly public. Intended to be witnessed by the largest numbers possible, they were scheduled for Dublin's market days — Wednesdays and Saturdays — to ensure 'a good turn out'.[51] The SCRAGBOY, or hangman, had no shortage of clients to dispatch to their eternal reward, for the ultimate penalty was imposed for everything from stealing a handkerchief to murder. Hangings reached their peak in 1786, to decline thereafter in the light of a change in government policy which eventually saw the opening of Dublin's 'Model Prison' of Mountjoy. The new institution was not slow to develop its own 'culture' and language. In 1862, Thomas Hanlon, a prisoner who had benefited from the JOY's educational regime, wrote in *An Essay on Slang or Counterfeit Language*:

> During my sojourn in this institution, I had from time to time to remark that among the majority of the inmates with whom I have been associated, there prevailed a fault, which degrades the character of him with whom it is predominant, as much as it hurts and irritates the feelings of those who meet its reproach ... for language is too exalted a term for such GIBBER-AGE ... slang is not only the sign of the vulgar, but of the blaguard and gail bird ...[52]

In the 1940s, in a series of articles in the magazine, *The Bell*, a prisoner, known only as 'D 83222', wrote of his incarceration; the articles were later published in book form.[53] On the morning in 1941 when Harry Gleeson was hanged in Mountjoy, 'every prisoner who retained a finer feeling or a semblance of sensibility shivered in his cell, while those old-timers who treated the tragic happening as an obscene joke, banging their stools against their cell doors, and shouting such cries as ONE OFF or ANOTHER FOR THE HIGH JUMP were the sewer rats of our economic latrines ...' Sensibility was perhaps more evident in the identification of the unfortunate victim as THE QUARE FELLA, the title of Brendan Behan's best-known play written when he himself was serving a sentence in the Joy. Throughout the action — set at the time of the execution of Bernard Kirwan in 1943 — a prisoner in the DIGGER or punishment cell, sings 'The Old Triangle'. 'THE OLD TRIANGLE was no myth,' according to Sean O'Briain: 'It was a large steel triangle hanging on a stand. Instead of using a bell, a warder struck it with a steel bar, and made it go "jingle jangle".'[54] During the Emergency, the Army mounted a guard at Mountjoy, 'where there were IRA men interned, as well as convicted prisoners. Many of the old soldiers were known as HEAD CASES due to their peculiar outlook ... one of them was on duty at THE HANGMAN'S POST, which covered the compound where the IRA men exercised.'[55]

'In the female prison/There are 70 women,/And 'tis there among them I'd like to be ...' The inmates of the Mountjoy women's prison shared, together with 'gear' and 'dust', a sense of identity:

> 'Ya have to have ya BORSTAL MARK but.'
> 'Me wha'?'
> 'Borstal mark, for Jasus' sake,' Rosie shouted. 'Ya deaf or wha'? Everyone that comes in here gets one'. Rosie pointed to a small black mark on her cheekbone.[56]

GANG WARFARE

There is a whole lexicon relating to drugs and drug abuse — amphs, crack, dike, doves, moggies, palf, naps, skunk, smack, to list a mere handful — but it is open to question how much of it has its roots in Dublin, apart from the drug gang names such as THE WESTIES and their adversaries: tough-looking plain-clothes detectives known as MOCKIES who may or may not be observed in a TWO-BULB, or squad car. On the other hand, the wider sphere of crime and its combatants have spawned a host of local nicknames — 'Self confessed crimelord Martin THE VIPER Foley will have to fork out around €200,000 in legal costs ...'[57] and, most notoriously, THE GENERAL, aka Martin Cahill. Ranged against him was 'the so-called TANGO SQUAD of elite Garda detectives [who] fought a war of attrition with the most colourful figure ever in Irish crime.'[58] Before them was the Dublin-based HEAVY GANG, allegedly a section of the Garda force who habitually dispensed with kid gloves, and before them again, the TWELVE APOSTLES, Michael Collins' War of Independence assassination squad which disposed of fourteen presumed British agents on what became known as Dublin's second BLOODY SUNDAY, 21 November 1920 (the first, 31 August 1913, was the occasion of rioting following the arrest of the labour leader, James Larkin).

STREET THEATRE

Street violence was apparently endemic, whether for political or simply social reasons. Bill Kelly witnessed a confrontation between two OUL WANS:

> ... they collided in mid-fight, claws grabbing for hair, eyes or clothing, as the neighbours tried to separate them, and word spread along the street like wildfire — RUGGY UP — and the crowds poured in from nowhere. It was cheap entertainment for the masses.[59]

Strikes not infrequently provoked serious violence, as in the case of the Lockout of 1913. Tram men who did not go on strike were subject to intimidation or worse. Two railway workers at Inchicore, who would normally have used the tram service to get home across the city, were obliged to make the long journey on foot, since those still working the trams were considered blacklegs, and a labour meeting scheduled for Inchicore Cross was almost certain to be broken up by the police:

'... An' I hate that bloody road on a wet night.'
'Me, too' (*pause*). 'To hell with them. I'm going by Inchicore Cross.'
'Sure, Sure. (*more briskly*). You'll be SHOEING A SHAFT, then?
'Aye.'
'Make it two.'

Shoeing a shaft was simple but uneconomic and illegal. It consisted of selecting a new sledge-hammer handle, a piece of hickory about four feet long. Shaped to the hand and thickened at one end. A short piece of iron piping was made red-hot, slid on to the thick end of the hammer-shaft and water-cooled into position ... Since a shod-shaft was a foot longer and a pound heavier than a constabulary baton, the Inchicore worthies often reached home almost undamaged.[60]

The establishment papers were quick to categorise the strikers: '... an attack was made on one of the tramcars at Arran Quay. The glass panelling of the car was smashed by missiles thrown by a group of TOUGHS on the sidewalk.'[61] The following year witnessed worse violence, British troops firing on a crowd at Bachelor's Walk in the wake of the Howth gun-running:

For a long time afterwards the raucous singing by Dublin urchins of a ballad which commemorated the event greeted the appearance of soldiers on the streets. It ran like this: 'We are the volunteers, the volunteers, the volunteers; we are the volunteers who fought the Scottish Borderers. Don't show your petticoats, your petticoats, your petticoats; Don't show your petticoats you dirty Scottish Borderers.'[62]

Some, however, could just not afford to be anti-British. 'We jeered at the SEPARATION WOMEN with their Union Jacks', C.S. Andrews recalled. 'The separation women were the wives of the soldiers in the British Army who lived on their separation allowances. They were very poor and were fanatically loyal to Britain.'[63]

JACKEENS OF ALL TRADES

Dublin is a city of vanished occupations. In the late 1700s, a Father Magulay lived in a large house at the end of Archibold's Court. According to Timothy Dawson, 'he was one of a few excommunicated Catholic priests known as COUPLE BEGGARS, who eked out an existence in the neighbourhood, principally by clandestine marriages ...'[64] 'At worst,' observed Toby Barnard, 'this illegal trade could bring a poor cleric to the scaffold, as it did the Dublin graduate, Edward Sewell, in 1740.'[65] By this time, the term 'undertaker' was replacing the traditional COFFIN-MAKER, but 'in 1895 a writer in a lady's magazine related how she and a companion were cheered on a winter's night "by the light from thirteen COFFIN SHOPS all clustered together at the end of the street [Cook Street]."'[66] The street at the time also housed a nailmaker and two rag merchants. The *Report of the Departmental Committee on Housing Conditions of the Working Class in the City of Dublin, 1914* listed among the 'Occupations of Families Occupying Tenement Houses in the City' those of Asphalter, Bellows Maker, Bell Ringer, Bird-Cage Maker, Bog Oak Carver, Boot Closer, Bung Maker, Carpet Planner, Chicken Butcher, Cockleman, Cork Sorter, Dock Policeman, Electric Plater, Fat Sorter, Feather

Cleaner, Fore Staller, Gut Cleaner, Horse Clipper, Legging Maker....
Few of the trades that employed 24,908 unskilled labourers in
1911 survive, and with them have vanished many of the words
and phrases peculiar to them. Their place has been taken by a
whole new range of employments and a vocabulary that is now
largely national or international – the language of Human
Resources, of bottom lines, down-sizing and, curiously enough in
an increasingly secular society, a substantial print-run of identi-
cal hymn-sheets. The immanence of such up-market employments has not, however, entirely inhibited the native flow of
Dublin wit: writing of the relatively new breed of political
reporters, Frank Dunlop observed 'incidentally, many of these
reporters were women - subsequently dubbed THE CLITORATI by the
inimitable P.J. Mara.'[67]

THIRST PRINCIPLES

The mechanisation of Dublin's dockland, for example, has seen
the extinguishing of a wide range of trades and practices:

> When the tub was filled [with coal] it was hooked to the crane's jib
> and the SINGER-OUT called out or sang out, 'Take it away, Charlie';
> The HOOKER-ON stood on the motor lorries, and risked his life every
> time a tub of coal swung to him to place on the lorry ...[68]

A dock-labourer's job depended upon being called at the daily
READING. (The word also carries a very different sense, that of the
reading of the names of perceived defaulters, moral or financial,
from the altar of a Catholic church. Thus HE READ ME [FROM A
HEIGHT]). The ordinary worker was thus at the mercy of the HEAD-
BUCKCAT or, as building-site ganger men were formerly known, THE
LAD WITH THE SHOUT. Back on the docks, those who were not CALLED
would 'run from one READ to another cause there'd be readings
for other ships. Like some of them we'd call CROSS-COUNTRY

RUNNERS cause they could run that fast to get to another read'.[69] Dockers — both employed and unemployed — would take a chance on finding a residue of stout in exported Guinness barrels returned 'empty' to City Quay. 'Now the HOGGERS — hoggers was men looking for free drink — they'd shake the barrels ... and hear it and say "We have one!".'[70] When the men sucked up the stout, they would be left with red mouths from the red RADDLE around the rim, a form of identification of the contents applied by a RADDLER, one of the many brewery trades. As well as drinking — it was thirsty work involving a morning 'tea-break' or BEERO HOUR — dockers were fond of betting: Willie Murphy recalled that every day his father 'had what they called a RAPPLE, a few bob — like you were betting tuppence and sixpence.'[71]

THREE QUOINS IN THE FOUNTAIN

BANANA BOAT, a term common in the printing trade in the days of hot metal, possibly had its origins in the docklands. According to Vinnie Caprani, who worked in the trade, it signified 'excessive, or lucrative, overtime working; double day shift etc ... it may also have come into vogue at the time of Harry Belafonte's mid-1950s record hit "The Banana Boat Song ..."'[72] Much of printers' long-established vocabulary was to vanish almost at a stroke with the abandonment of hot metal consequent upon the intro-duction of electronics: DRAGON'S BLOOD, a preparation employed in blockmaking; FLONG, a flexible material used in newspaper print-ing on cylinder presses; SPIDER'S WEMIX, denoting an additive for softening printing ink; and QUOINS, devices for locking type into the chase. More general terms were LASH-IN — a celebratory pub get-together to welcome an apprentice newly 'out of his time'; SERGEANT MAJOR, 'good copies of jobbing work put at the top of a pile to create a good impression, especially if the rest of the job is of inferior quality because of offset, poor alignment, etc.'[73] One of the old type-sizes in use before the general adoption of the point system, Nonpareil, was invariably NOM'PRULL in Dublin pronunciation. HEAD MONEY, the printing term for trade union dues, may have derived from the eighteenth-century practice of printers meeting each Saturday night in the Brazen Head and Carteret Head inns to transact union business.

DOCKED PAY

Permanent, pensionable jobs — the 'job for life' — were, of course, in great demand. "'O'Hara seems to be in a bad way. What's he doing?" "Nothing", said Little Chandler. "He's gone to the dogs." "But Hogan has A GOOD SIT, hasn't he?" "Yes; he's in the Land Commission"'.[74] Printing was a long-established and highly regulated trade, carrying a degree of social distinction; but for many of those who were not ON THE LABOUR — recipients of the dole or SCRATCH — a job, any job, particularly in the early years of the twentieth century, was something to be hung on to at all costs, with the constant fear of summary dismissal for what would now be considered very minor offences. Seán O'Casey 'didn't feel comfortable on his way to work the following morning. He was almost sure to GET HIS DOCKET. Well, if he did aself [itself], he'd stick it out like a man ...'[75] The picture was different for the securely self-employed, but some relied on 'HITTING AND TIPPING — doing bits of jobs around the place, nothing permanent — knocking down hedges for farmers, that kind of thing.'[76] Failing all else, there was emigration, but even before the era of the Green Card, this was not entirely plain sailing. 'Someone had to claim you and you had to DO A CONSUL. Doing a consul involved visiting the American embassy and having a medical examination.'[77] But 'sons and daughters went out of every family. Those who remained behind awaited those essential remittances known as the AMERICAN POST.'[78]

PAY BACK

For those who did remain, working conditions, particularly in traditional areas of employment such as transport and the docks, left much to be desired, and frequent strikes and threats of strikes brought workers and the struggling unions into confrontation with the employers, with the constant risk of scab or FREE labour being brought in. In 1908, when the dockers handling coal refused to work with non-union labour, the National Union of Dock Labourers warned: 'Unemployed men, keep away from the harbour of Dublin. Don't scab on your fellow countrymen who are locked out by the employers. Don't CAREY.' James Carey was the informer who betrayed his comrades involved in the Phoenix Park assassinations of 1881. When in the same year the maltsters came out for higher wages — they worked a seven-day week from 6 am to 6 pm for 16 shillings — they demanded the abolition of 'the BACK SHILLING, whereby the employer retained that sum each week until the end of the working season, it being returned if the conduct was satisfactory'.[79] UNDER THE HAMMER was in common use in the coal yards to describe men who did not earn the minimum wage.

The various branches of the clothing trade offered what were considered at the time as 'respectable' occupations, though with equally poor financial returns. Many drapers' assistants came from beyond the Pale. 'For many of them the LIVING-IN system (i.e. sleeping accommodation on employers' premises) was common down to 1910.'[80] Cobblers were WAXIES,. from the waxed thread they employed, and they organised an annual outing, or WAXIES' DARGLE, to the River Dargle in Ringsend. Patrick F. Byrne recalled an old man telling him of 'an apparition known as LARRY THE WAX (a cobbler in his lifetime), who appeared somewhere around the Liberties, and who disappeared if anyone told him to "go to hell"'.[81] Another long-established and respected trade was that of signwriter, a calling which caused some confusion at a meeting between the writer and editor, John Ryan, and a crony of Brendan Behan's father, Stephen:

I asked him did he know the Behan boys ... to make it easier to distinguish him and because he had already had some small pieces in Irish published I referred to him as 'Brendan, you know, the writer'. 'The WRITER?' he queried in surprise. 'There's only one writer in that family and that's the father, Stephen. Did you ever see the sign for Guinness he done up there on the gable over Slattery's in Phibsboro?'[82]

SHE WHEELED HER WHEELBARROW

There were far worse jobs: among them that which was still known in Australia into the 1950s as a 'sanitary carter'.

'Johnny Casside, Johnny Casside, your mother wants you quick! Th' DUNG-DODGERS are here!' Johnny hated these dirt-hawks who came at stated times to empty out the PETTIES and ash-pits in the back yards of the people, filling the whole place with a stench that didn't disappear for a week.[83]

When the unpopular slum rehousing programme began in the 1930s, a somewhat more hygienic variant of the dung-dodger made his appearance 'threatening the very existence of the community. He wore a rain-coat, glasses, rode a bike and was called the SANITARY MAN – a name synonymous with pimp, ponce, or PROSTITUTE'S BANNER-MAN.'[84] TUGGERS, invariably women, went round collecting old clothes in exchange for cheap delft. The term SHAWLIE, or SHAWL, originally a female fishmonger *à la* Molly Malone, was subsequently applied to women street-sellers in general: 'Blind to the world up in a sheebeen in Bride Street ... fornicating with two shawls and a BULLY [protector of prostitutes] on guard.'[85] In the early 1920s, May Bannon worked for the Dublin Box Company. 'Following pregnancies spent working a BANGER — a mechanical stitching machine in widespread use in the trade — May's children came forth "black and blue".'[86] In the first decade of the last century, *The Irish Worker* was urging the women in the labour force to relieve themselves of the burden of housework.

> Walls were to be covered with paint, not paper, floors to be stripped and left bare, and household linen reduced to essentials ... 'With all this BROKERAGE cast away, most of the curtains disposed of, and the brass and steel ornaments sold to the antique man, we lighten the household work.'[87]

PROPER ORDER

The domestic scene has changed, if not in the manner *The Irish Worker* recommended, and with the changes another large compendium of Dublinese has gone for its tea. The Latvian nanny gets the job of POSSING OUT the floor; the apron as a fashion statement has replaced the CROSSOVER BIB; the COFFIN-ROLLER (mangle) has given way to the washing machine; and with the advent of the 'ensuite', no longer do we resort to the TWISS to do our PEETNEY. The utensil thus named was a backhanded compliment to a visiting Englishman, Dr Richard Twiss, who, arriving in Ireland towards the end of the eighteenth century, did not endear himself to the citizens by his outspoken comments on the country and its mores. Shortly after his visit, a Dublin manufacturer of chamber pots printed his portrait on the bottom of a range of his products with the accompanying verse:

> Here you may behold a liar
> Well deserving of hell-fire:
> Everyone who likes may p----
> Upon the learned Doctor T----.

PIGEON ENGLISH

Filing cabinets, filing pedestals, modern office bookcases, Office tables & computer tables, stationary cupboards & stationary shelving . . . office partition work systems, steel office safes (8), stationary pigeon holes.

Auction advertisement, Herman & Wilkinson, Rathmines Road, *Irish Independent*, 20 August 2005

Most self-respecting Dublin printing houses, before the craft of metal type was swept away, employed an individual whose sole task it was to sit in a little room, reading proofs. Little or nothing escaped his (invariably) eagle eye. The same could be said for the men who, installed at their huge, clanking composing machines, Monotype, Linotype, Intertype, transferred into slugs or characters of metal — a necromancer's amalgam of lead, tin and antimony — the words on the written or typewritten page of 'copy'. These men — again invariably men — had frequently forgotten more about spelling, grammar and syntax than was ever in the possession of the originators of the manuscripts or typescripts; and they were far from backward in displaying their verbal as well as their digital skills.

No more. With everyone now his or her own proofreader, or so it would seem, it is not surprising that the old disciplines are falling apart at the seams. It may not matter all that much, if all you are trying to do is to sell holes for stationary pigeons, but in the larger perspective, it constitutes a display of wilful ignorance or, *in extremis*, serious confusion. At the last presidential election, RTÉ's *Morning Ireland* programme informed its listeners that the low turnout was in part attributable to areas of 'high unemployment' and SOCIAL DEPRAVITY — an interesting sociological discovery, to say the least; we are over-familiar with those despicable EX-PATRIOTS, only one step removed from common informers, who go off to live in foreign countries. *The Irish Times* programme guide reminded us that 'the brand new series of 'ER' slipped into the RTÉ1 Sunday night schedules in December without any fanfare — and then, weirdly, BREAKED for Christmas ...'[1] Weirdly indeed. Freudian slips flap in the wind: 'Well, Brown and his colleagues were making further observations in order to confirm things and to provide a fuller picture before going PUBIC.'[2] At times, it would seem, we take endless trouble to get it wrong. As Gavin Corbett observed (in two senses of the word):

> Above a certain garage, on a certain busy street in northside Dublin, resides the most sandwich-dropping example of pollutant punctuation that I'm aware of ... the third word in the sign above the garage is CAR'S (*sic*). The most frightening thing about this particular piece of public illiteracy, as a friend recently pointed out to me, is that the letters and superfluous apostrophe used to make up the sign are three-dimensional, bolt-on objects. In other words, that apostrophe used to make up the sign was not the result of an idle stroke of a paintbrush — somebody actually thought it needed to be there, budgeted for it, and went to the trouble of writing 'Apostrophe: x 1' on an order form.[3]

The greengrocer's plural, as it has been called, has been with us a long time, as have other common and well-rehearsed confusions such as militate/mitigate, faze/phase and so on. 'I try to avoid sounding like Jeremy Clarkson or a member of the grumpy old man tendency,' says Michael Williams, writing on 'a particularly hideous form of newspeak' in his 'Readers' Editor' column.[4] So, does it matter that, having failed abysmally in the matter of the first national language, we are in the process, in this era of educated illiteracy, of confining the second to the dustbin of degraded usage? And what, if anything, has it got to do with Dublinese?

DOWN IN THE DUMPS

Frank Farrell, in a letter to *The Irish Times,* took that paper to task for its 'misuse of words':

> ... what are we to make of it when Dick Roche goes horsing around Wicklow vales in pursuit of the REMEDIATION of illegal dumps (front-page report, May 3)? Worst of all, where are we left if *The Irish Times* unblushingly endorses his pretensions without so much as a *sic* or even an inverted comma?[5]

This is not a matter of senile grumpiness or proscriptive pedantry: *remediation* is not a word in any accepted or acceptable sense. It is a confusion of *mediate* and *remedy,* and as a coinage it fails the basic criterion of conveying a clear and unequivocal meaning. It is fortuitously obscurantist, as opposed to the type of newspeak that deliberately sets out to obscure its meaning for a variety or reasons. And this latter area of jargon is becoming as much a facet of Dublinese — one might term it Corporate Dublinese — as the strangled diphthongs of Dortspeak. The 'Current Account' column in the business section of *The Irish Times* featured Donal O'Mahony, who 'produces a regular comment on debt markets for Davy Stockbrokers ...'[6] The Bank of England's Monetary Policy Committee, he was quoted as saying, has 'become an eminently predictable beast in recent years, cor-ralling most of its recent activism into predesignated months ... the greater potency of incremental policy adjustments in a more leveraged economic environment speaks first and foremost to the UK consumer whose debt/income ratio remains a tad stratospheric.' It would not be so bad, perhaps, if this kind of stuff remained within the glass-fronted grottoes of the Financial Services Centre. 'People increasingly now talk that language of their workplace,' observes the Australian writer, Don Watson: 'which is this managerial speak. I'm sure in some houses they're talking about proactively oversizing the porridge.'[7]

TENSE SITUATION

As in business, so in politics. Political Dublinese, as David Robbins diagnoses it, increasingly has recourse to 'our old friend, the Celtic Conditional', illustrating it with a quote from a spokesman for a helicopter company to the effect that 'most of our customers WOULD BE businessmen'.[8] 'They "would be business-men" if what?' he asks: 'If they had studied Commerce at UCD? If they had followed daddy into the family firm? If they had any entrepreneurial acumen?' He goes on to point out:

Liam Lawlor spent months in this strange tense during the Flood Tribunal. Liam Lawlor wouldn't have done this and wouldn't have done that, he whined daily. Lawlor is a master of the Celtic Conditional, and refined it into a sub-category, the Hiberno Hypothetical. What the Tribunal is saying couldn't be true, he implied, because Liam Lawlor (he likes to refer to himself in the third person) had done that, he wouldn't have done this ...

These manifestations, and others like them, characterise the speech habits of the new urban elite, those whom the economist

David Williams, who is credited with coining the term CELTIC TIGER (though it has been pre-dated by some to 1994), describes as THE POPE'S CHILDREN, the generation conceived in the stimulating circumstances of John Paul II's visit in 1979. 'McWilliams calls the new upper class HIBERNO COSMOPOLITANISTS, or HICO's,' explained Kathy Sheridan.[9] 'The centre of their universe is Ranelagh Triangle ...' Dublin 6 supplanting Dublin 4?

OUTER LIMITS

The inference is that the days when Rawthmines and Rawthgar, and, trotting behind them, Ranelagh, constituted a small if influential linguistic and phonetic nucleus are long gone. All evidence points to the fact that the idiom and accidence of the capital in its various manifestations is spreading like wild rhubarb in Achill. The Kildare accent, for example, is seriously under threat. 'The accents of Wicklow and Louth are also endangered,' according to Kim Bielenberg, 'while that noted SLURRY MUNCHER, Navan Man, has been labelled a MUPPET and told to GET OUTTA DAT GARDEN (cop on to himself).'[10] Shane Hegarty observes: 'It is sobering to realise that within a decade most of Dublin will, in fact, consist of housing estates in Wicklow.'[11] In the light of these demographic shifts, Dublinese, both that of the political, cultural and managerial élite and, more generally, modified Dortspeak, is approaching, or aspiring to the status of a national norm. According to Flann Ó Riain:

> ... the current 'in' accent increasingly used by radio and television presenters and personalities and that used by actors in radio and television commercials, is that of the better-off 'upper-class' minority based in Dublin, and of a percentage of country persons imitating them.[12]

There is some way to go, probably, before this mode of speech achieves the acceptance accorded to the so-called Received Pronunciation in British English, but the signs are there, and the pervasiveness of the Dublin-based media, both print and broadcast, will ensure that the process, if ultimately constrained or the subject of a cultural backlash, is unlikely to be effectively halted in its tracks.

NAME CALLING

'As heard in the formal language of the national radio station, Radio Telefís Éireann, only occasional items of lexicon (e.g. *taoiseach* ...) distinguish it from Standard English,' claimed the linguist David Crystal.[13] If that were ever true, it is true no longer. But it is those who speak the words, rather than the words themselves, who seem to account for a constant element of listener dissatisfaction. 'Does anyone actually *audition* anyone any more, or even *interview* them before allowing them on air?' protested the veteran broadcaster Gay Byrne. 'Does anyone care?'[14] It is difficult to believe that anyone does when, for example, virtually every Frenchman named Jean is obliged to undergo a sex-change to Jeanne, or 'déjà-vu' consistently emerges as DÉJÀ VOUS (you already?) — though perhaps the latter can be accepted as anglicised. (After all, if we burden the French with 'Agence de Relooking', a service to advise on one's personal and professional image, we must suffer something in return.) 'I find it grating on the ears to hear RTÉ's sports commentators regularly mispronouncing the names of two world-class Spanish golfers — Olazábal and Jiménez,' complained F. Cronin. 'The emphasis is on the syllables that have the accents. It's not rocket science.'[15] Stuart Murray, writing to the same paper, simply wanted the station to decide whether its own name should be pronounced ARE TEE EEE, AAH TEE EE, ORR TEE EE, URR TEE EE, 'or some other variation'.[16]

RYNDABYTE ROUTE

Whilst such protestations might be dismissed as the obsessions of fuddy-duddy *Irish Times*' readers and the contemporary manifestations of 'Pro Bono Publico' or 'Mother of Ten', there is evidence of a wider unease based on the belief that Dublin, with the connivance of the national broadcaster, is engaged in a policy of linguistic attrition. If the jokes about the AA Roadwatch accent have become somewhat tired, the impression persists that that organisation exercises some kind of positive discrimination in favour of the Dort accent, even though it is ostensibly addressing a nationwide audience. Thus 'county' is invariably CANTY, or a near phonetic equivalent, and 'town' TAYN, whilst its announcers exhibit a remarkable unfamiliarity with or indifference to the pronunciation of place names beyond the Pale, to the extent that it can be only a matter of time before we are advised of tailbacks in At Henry. The stress is placed more and more on the first syllable, whether locally customary or not (BANbridge; TULLAmore; LISmore — the citizens of the eponymous town in New South Wales would be sympathetic). In fairness, the traditional Dublin pronunciations of CapEL and WestMOREland Streets are largely preserved. 'Why does RTÉ choose persons with non-Irish accents,' complains Flann Ó Riain, 'many indeed with no knowledge of Irish, and thereby incapable of correctly pronouncing Irish words, phrases and terms?'[17] Whilst it would be flying in the face of linguistic rectitude to describe the Dort accent as 'non-Irish', his point is well made.

GIVE US OUR BREAD ON A DAILY BASIS ...

RTÉ is, of course, an easy target, in this as in other contexts, but it is open to question whether it is actively promoting neo-Dublinese or simply reflecting a wider trend. 'Nowhere has our culture taken a greater hammering than in the spoken word,' according to Michael Clifford:

The Irish no longer speak in a manner rooted to the soil. That's so yesterday. Instead we gabber in American, with or without tears. Everything is, like, so cool. Everybody is a guy. Only some know where it's at. When required, they step up to the plate. They cut to the chase to beat the band. Have a nice day is just around the corner. You get the picture?[18]

But we cannot blame the Americans for all the clichés that litter our speech — the 'basically' that shreds every sentence, the 'absolutely' which has supplanted the simple 'yes' to the extent that one is tempted to rewrite Joyce: '... so that he could feel my breasts all perfume and absolutely his heart was going like mad and absolutely I said absolutely I will absolutely'. These examples, of course, constitute adopted rather than generic Dublin speech — if the distinction may still validly be made — just part of the whole tedious business of going forward through a window of opportunity to a soft landing on a level playing field. But are there any really home-grown Dublin clichés?

At 10.25 I asked a bus inspector if the timetable had any basis in reality.
He cheerily answered: 'Ah, sure it's Sunday morning. You KNOW YOURSELF.'[19]

Then there is the RARE OUL' TIMES, of course. And, perhaps, the CÚPLA FOCAL (often mis-spelt, 'focail': 'cúpla' takes the singular). And, thanks to Gay Byrne, there's ONE FOR EVERYBODY IN THE AUDIENCE. Deriving similarly from the broadcast media, STOP THE LIGHTS! is expressive of concern or surprise. From a 1970s television quiz show, it has been absorbed into the vernacular. A SIX-MARKER, from the 1940s *Question Time*, has similarly outlived its origins.

UP DOWN UNDER

There is another imported speech pattern identified particularly with neo-Dublinese. 'Upspeak is a communication device employed by people who've watched one too many episodes of *Sex and the City* ... or *Friends*,' according to Conor Behan. 'They make questions out of sentences that really shouldn't be questions in the first place. Or more simply they speak "up" at the end of a sentence and turn that sentence into a question.'[20] But whereas Behan blames the Americans, others, as has been said, identify Australian soaps such as *Neighbours* as the source of the infection. The rising inflexion is indeed a characteristic of Australian speech but Padraig McCarthy, in a letter to *The Irish Times*, pointed out that it is common in south County Wicklow and in County Cork and elsewhere. 'Could it be an export from Ireland to those antipodean climes?' he asks.[21] Indeed it could, and it is only one example of such exports being returned with interest. But Conor Behan, contributing to the regular column, 'Teen Times', is not to be consoled:

> What's happened to our individuality? I don't mean the usual teenage 'individuality' of having long hair and only listening to music with lots of screaming and guitars ... it's about time we stopped and realised the absolutely ridiculous way many people are talking. It's silly and it laughs in the face of the fact that we're Irish.[22]

Interestingly, it would appear from this that uneasiness in the face of current developments in Dublinese is not confined to the grumpy old men. Molly McCloskey wrote:

> This morning, I woke up to a Vodafone ad in which two young Irish women say things such as 'Loser!' [rising inflexion on the second syllable] and 'It's like ... €5 cheaper? [Valley-girl pause between 'like' and 'five'; a statement voiced as a question]. It

occurred to me that if the Government want to preserve eth-
nically specific verbal dexterity, it may have to begin subsidis-
ing it.[23]

There was a time when there was a more or less clear phonetic
distinction between the voices employed in radio and television
commercials, 'vibrant with insincerity' as the cliché had it, and
the normal run of programming. Now the so-called mid-Atlantic
accent is common to both, and since the majority of radio commercials at least are Dublin-originated, Dortspeak is increasingly
in evidence. Extra-Pale accents tend to be employed largely in
comic contexts.

STREET WISE

In the summer of 2005, a controversy developed over the
naming or renaming of Dublin streets, with particular reference to
the Irish-language versions. Writing in *History Ireland*, Patrick
Garry argued that Dublin City Council's publication, *Dublin
Streetnames/Sráidainmneacha Bhaile Átha Cliath*, had 'an error
rate of over 20 per cent and even includes names that do not
exist. Where are Árd Ró Street and Árd Ró Place?'[24] Citing as an
example the proposal to replace the name *Sráid Thobar Phádraig*
with *Sráid Nassau* (the name in English is Nassau Street), he
argued, quoting other instances, that 'the streets of Dublin are
being systematically sanitised of their heritage and culture ...
The threat to our street names is serious, and if old names are
allowed to disappear a gross act of cultural vandalism will have
been perpetrated on the citizens of Dublin — the textual version
of the Wood Quay débâcle.'

He was answered by Pádraig Ó Cearbhaill of the Department
of Community, Rural and Gaeltacht Affairs, who produced historical and toponymic evidence for several of the proposed
changes, specifically in the case of Nassau Street, suggesting, in

part, that 'Nassau was first used in 1749 when Lord Molesworth
gave the name to the street in honour of his son Richard Nassau ...'
and that

> ... as the identification of St Patrick's Well Lane with Nassau
> Street alone is incorrect and as the change in nomenclature
> mooted over 80 years ago to Tubber Patrick Street was
> rejected, what purpose does the Irish form of the last-men-
> tioned name serve, i.e. *Sráid Thobar Phádraig*, other than its
> avoidance of an eighteenth-century aristocratic name of
> foreign origin and its commemoration of a former holy well?
> With reference to the latter point, is the Irish-language
> version of a street name the appropriate means of commemo-
> rating such a location?[25]

LACKING MUSSEL

To which one is prompted to return an answer in the affirmative.
There would seem to be no good reason, historical, linguistic or
otherwise, why bilingual street names should set out to be exact
translations or renditions one of the other. The two languages,
even if they appear on the same sign, are by definition mutually
exclusive, drawing from different traditions and etymologies.
Why then should the two be brought into a forced coherence,
destroying in the process a name which, whether historically
well-grounded or not, is a significant element in the verbal landscape of the city? The former Bord Fáilte was never, in English,
the Welcome Board or even the Board of Welcome; the Tánaiste
is not commonly referred to in English as the Tanist; Córas
Iompair Éireann has rarely been rendered as the Irish Transport
System. And if you are going to rename *Sráid Tréanlámhach*
Sráid Armstrong, on account of a questionable authentication,
you might just as well not bother with the 'Irish' version at all.
At a time when traditional Dublin nomenclature is vanishing in

both languages — pints of Diageo, An Lár giving way to City Centre — this politically correct approach to the city's street names would appear to be lacking both in sensitivity and respect. 'There are lovely street names that can be used in Irish or even in English, like Mussel Lane of Skinners' Row,' claimed National Museum Director Pat Wallace, 'that tell you what work was done there in the past. Is it that we are all too grand now or too posh for these kinds of names? Or is it that we are insecure?'[26] North Brunswick Street, for example, 'was formerly Channel Row, a name which is still retained in the Irish Version Rae na Canálach'.[27] And Shane Hegarty suggested that as Dublin oozes out over the surrounding countryside, 'developers attempt to soften the environment by harking back to the area's pastoral past and giving the new roads names such as the Vale, the Meadow, the Hillock … Of course, celebrating the present rather than the past would be far less marketable. Nobody wants to live at 23 Concrete Jungle.'[28]

GETTING THE BUS TO WARSAW

'Trouble with this country there's too many dagoes in it. Takin' the bread an' butter outa the mouths of our wives an' children. Can't even speak English. Don' wanna speak English. Yabber, yabber, yabber. That's all they do. Yabber, yabber, yabber … You gunna let 'em talk that stuff out here? Dagoes an' Jerries an' Balts an' Poles an' Lithu-bloody-wanians?'[29]

Australia began its move towards a multicultural society 50 years ago with the arrival of a steady stream of immigrants from mainland Europe. The impact on a society which had until then been overwhelmingly Anglo-Celtic (if you except the dinkum Aussies who had been around for some 60,000 years) was to be far-reaching and controversial. The reaction of the drunk in the Sydney train as portrayed by Nino Culotta, himself one of the early arrivals, was not untypical, and 'non-nationals' can still be picked upon by chauvinistic elements of the old order, even though the street names in Melbourne may be bilingual in English and Greek, and Italian the *lingua franca* on Sydney's Parramatta Road. Although for anyone who has been familiar with the country over the course of the years, the cultural and social changes are strikingly apparent, there is less evidence of linguistic overspill: the Australian language remains largely as it was before the 1950s witnessed the arrival of the 'New Australians' — a term of the time not without its derogatory overtones.

GO ON, GO ON, GO ON ...

Half a century on, Ireland in general, and its capital in particular, is confronted with a similar demographic development; and if the social implications are beyond the scope of this enquiry, it will be interesting to see what impact, if any, the languages of the wide variety of New Dubs will have upon the established idiom. As yet, of course, there is little evidence: 'Joyous [a Nigerian lady] was good at explaining how immigrant women would get social welfare (DE SOCIAL) and how to fill in the forms correctly ...'[30] but that hardly constitutes a major contribution to the vernacular. Dublinese, however, has a long history of mopping up linguistic spillage, and there is no reason to suppose that the process will not continue, though to what extent and in what directions it is probably futile to speculate. As the Australian lexicographer Sidney Baker put it:

> The extent to which a country absorbs the language of another country is not governed by lexicographers or academics ... The instinct of the people as a whole governs it. They accept what they like, they reject completely words which have no useful application or which do not appeal to them, they modify others.[31]

Brendan Killeen, in his 'Letter from Copenhagen', characterised such national individuality:

> We don't speak — we communicate through a 'half-talk code of mysteries, the wink-and-elbow language of delight', as Kavanagh called it. 'Will you have a cup of tea?' asks person A putting on the kettle. 'No, I'm in a terrible hurry,' says person B taking off their coat. 'A half-cup then,' says person A. That conversation would make no sense to a Dane.[32]

And he sounds a note of warning: 'Ireland, watch out, immigration is a fact of life and we can learn a lot from Denmark. Rather than attempting to reduce a rainbow of nationalities to a monotone of green, maybe we should consider adding a few tones to what it means to be Irish.' On the evidence of the centuries, and in spite of the progressive levelling of dialect and discourse throughout the Anglophone global suburb, it would seem likely that the expanding capital, 'this arrogant city' as the poet Donagh MacDonagh described it, will retain and enhance its cherished ability to define, redefine and describe the world very much in its own terms.

ENDNOTES

Note: Books, newspapers, periodicals etc. are Dublin-published unless otherwise stated.

Chapter 1: FROM THE DANES TO TODAY (PP. 1–23)
1   Referring to accounts of the riot over Synge's *Playboy,* Terry Eagleton (*The Irish Times,* 25 June 2005) suggests that 'this, like Stephen Dedalus's reference to the tundish ... is a topic which should surely be subject to rigorous state censorship for the next half-century ...'
2   Oliver St John Gogarty, *As I was Going Down Sackville Street* (London 1936).
3   Gene Kerrigan, *Another Country* (1998).
4   Anne Simpson, *Blooming Dublin* (Edinburgh 1991).
5   Vincent Caprani, *Vulgar Verse & Variations, Rowdy Rhymes & Rec-im-itations* (1987).
6   Richard Stanihurst in Raphael Holinshed, *Chronicles of England, Scotland and Ireland* (1577).
7   Kenneth Jackson, 'The Celtic Languages during the Viking Period', *Proceedings of the International Congress of Celtic Studies, 1959* (1962).
8   Fynes Morrison, *An Itinerary containing his ten year's travel (1617)* (Glasgow 1907-8).
9   Alan Bliss (ed.), *A Dialogue in Hybernian Stile between A & B and Irish Eloquence, by Jonathan Swift* (1977).
10 Charles Macklin, *The True-Born Irishman* (1793).
11 Thomas Sheridan, *A Course of Lectures on Elocution* (London 1762).
12 Richard Brinsley Sheridan, *The Rivals* (London 1775).
13 Samuel A. Ossory Fitzpatrick, *Dublin, A Historical and Topographical Account of the City* (1907).
14 P.W. Joyce, *English as we speak it in Ireland* (1910).
15 Alan Bliss, 'The Emergency of Modern English Dialects in Ireland', in Diarmaid Ó Muirithe ed., *The English Language in Ireland* (Dublin & Cork 1977).
16 Dominic Behan, *Teems of Times and Happy Returns* (London 1961).
17 Mary Hannigan and Gerry Thornley, *The Irish Times,* 18 October 2005.
18 Diarmuid Doyle 'Teanga ag disappearing suas its own poll cháca go dtí an exclusion of others', *Sunday Tribune,* 19 December 2004.
19 *The Irish Times,* 12 April 1953.
20 Myles na gCopaleen, *The Irish Times,* 13 April 1953.
21 *Suaimhneas,* peace, tranquillity; *Aisling,* vision; *Fáilte,* welcome; *Suantraí,* lullaby; *Gleoite,* lovely; *Dreoilín,* wren; *Síosarnach,* rustling sound; *Deora Dé,* fuchsia; *Bothántaíocht,* visiting houses for pastime or gossip; *Sceitimíní,* excitement.
22 Stephen Collins, *The Power Game* (2004).
23 *The Irish Times,* 5 November 2004.
24 Sarah McInerney, *Sunday Tribune,* 5 February 2004.
25 *Sunday Business Post,* 31 July 2005.
26 C.S. Andrews, *Dublin Made Me* (Dublin/Cork 1979).
27 *The Irish Times,* 20 August 2005.
28 John Boland, *Irish Independent,* 6 August 2005.
29 'Bertie's Blog', *Sunday Tribune,* 24 April 2005.
30 István Bart, *Hungary and the Hungarians* (Budapest 2002).
32 Gerry O'Flaherty, *Ireland of the Welcomes,* January/February 1975.

33   *The Irish Times*, 15 November1997.
34   See Bernard Share, *Slanguage, A Dictionary of Slang and Colloquial English in Ireland.* 2nd ed. (2003).
34   *The Irish Times*, 26 January 2002.
35   Seamus Martin, *The Irish Times*,1995.
36   *Sunday Tribune*, 21 June 1998.
37   *Village*, Dublin, 17 June 2005.
38   Tom Corkery, *Tom Corkery's Dublin (*1980).
39   O'Flaherty, op cit.
40   Joyce, op cit.
41   Hugh Leonard, *Plays and Players* (London, May 1964).
42   Diarmaid Ó Muirithe, *The Words We Use* (1996).
43   Joyce, op cit.
44   *Sunday Business Post*, 18 March 2001.
45   *Irish Press*, 21 November 1966.
46   Ibid.
47   Vincent Caprani, *A Walk Around Dublin* (Belfast 1992).
48   Brendan Behan, *Moving Out* (*The Complete Plays of Brendan Behan*, London, 1978).
49   Bryan MacMahon, 'Brendan Behan: Vital Human Being – a Memoir, *North American Review*, Summer 1964.
50   Myles na gCopaleen, *The Best of Myles* (London 1968).
51   *The Irish Times*, 4 June 2005.
52   Quoted by Kim Bielenberg, *Irish Independent*, 27 August 2005.

Chapter 2: THE WORD ON THE STREETS (PP. 24–62)
1   Memories are short: the Spike was the South Dublin Union Workhouse, otherwise THE PAUPERS or the UNMARRIED MOTHERS.
2   *The Irish Times*, 15 March 1999.
3   After the comedian Jimmy O'Dea's character 'Mrs Mulligan the Pride of the Coombe'.
4   *Sunday Tribune*, 6 December 1998.
5   *The Irish Times*, 23 November 2003.
6   *The Bell*, December 1944.
7   James Joyce, *Ulysses* (London 1936).
8   Austin Clarke, *Twice Around the Black Church* (London 1962).
9   Myles na gCopaleen, *The Irish Times*, 13 April 1953.
10   Quidnunc, *The Irish Times*, 1953.
11   Vincent Caprani, *Vulgar Verse & Variations. Rowdy Rhymes & Recimitations* (1987).
12   *The Irish Times*, 15 August 2005.
13   Ibid., 29 December 2001.
14   Éamonn MacThomáis, *Janey Mack, me Shirt is Black* (1982).
15   *The Irish Times*, 25 August 2004.
16   Ibid., 30 December 2002.
17   Alex Findlater, *Findlaters* (2001).
18   Samuel Lewis, *The Topographical Dictionary of Ireland* (London 1837).
19   Santo Cilauro, Tom Gleisner and Rob Sitch, *Molvania (Jetlag travel guide)* (London 2004).
20   Brendan Behan, *Moving Out*, op. cit.
21   *The Irish Times*, 19 March 2005.
22   John Edward Walsh, *Ireland Sixty Years Ago* (1847).
23   *The Irish Times*, 25 April 2006.
24   *The Irish Times*, 20 August 2005.
25   *Sunday Tribune*, 19 September 2004.
26   Ibid.
27   Ibid., 30 January 2005.
28   'An Outsider Southsider', *The Irish Times*, 9 April 2005.
29   *The Irish Star*, 19 October 1994.
30   *Sunday Tribune*.

31   *The Irish Times,* 12 March 2005.
32   Vincent Caprani, 'Raytown', *Cara,* March–April 1988.
33   See Maria and Richard Lovell Edgeworth, *An Essay on Irish Bulls* (London 1802).
34   *The Irish Times.*
35   Ibid.
36   *Sunday Tribune,* 27 March 2005.
37   *The Irish Times,* 12 August 2004.
38   *Irish Independent,* 18 September 2003.
39   Séamus de Burca, 'Growing up in Dublin', *Dublin Historical Record,* June 1976.
40   *Sunday Tribune,* 22 January 2006.
41   Christopher FitzSimon, *The Boys* (1994).
42   *The Irish Times,* 4 December 1930.
43   James Plunkett, *Farewell Companions* (London 1977).
44   Willie Murphy, quoted in Kevin C. Kearns, *Dublin Street Life and Lore* (1991).
45   Rose Doyle, *Trade Names* (2004).
46   Walsh, op. cit.
47   *The Irish Times,* 13 March 1931.
48   Patrick F. Byrne, 'Ghosts of Old Dublin', *Dublin Historical Record,* December 1976.
49   T. Dawson, 'Between the Steps', *Dublin Historical Record,* June 1971.
50   Anto Byrne, 'Diary of a Dublin Football Fan', *Sunday Tribune,* 14 June 1998.
51   T. Dawson, 'Of Cooks and Coffin Makers', *Dublin Historical Record,* June 1977.
52   Brian Mac Giolla Phádraig, 'Dublin One Hundred Years Ago', *Dublin Historical Record,*
      December 1969.
53   *The Irish Times,* 23 February 2004.
54   Plunkett, op. cit.
55   *Dublin Historical Record,* September 1955.
56   C.S. Andrews, *Dublin Made Me,* op. cit.
57   Austin Clarke, op. cit.
58   Anthony Cronin, *Dead as Doornails* (Dublin & London, 1976; revised ed. Dublin, 1999).
59   Edgar F. Keatinge, 'Colourful, Tuneful Dublin', *Dublin Historical Record,* September–
      November 1947.
60   Theophilus Cibber, *Epistle to Mr Warburton* (London 1753).
61   Ibid.
62   Quoted in Jim Cooke, *Ireland's Premier Coachbuilder* (n.d.).
63   *Dublin Evening Post,* 4 February 1826.
64   Frank Hopkins, *Rare Old Dublin* (Cork 2002).
65   Joyce, op. cit.
66   Moira Lysaght, 'My Dublin', *Dublin Historical Record,* September 1977.
67   Michael Corcoran, *Through Streets Broad and Narrow* (Leicester 2000).
68   Andrews, op. cit.
69   Lysaght, op. cit.
70   *No More Peasants,* BBC broadcast, 22 August 1948.
71   Máirín Johnston, *Around the Banks of Pimlico* (1985).
72   John Mannion, quoted in Kearns, op. cit.
73   Corcoran, op. cit.
74   Seán O'Casey, *Pictures in the Hallway* (London 1963).
75   *The Irish Times,* 13 July 2005.
76   Seán O'Casey, *I Knock at the Door* (London 1939).
77   Bob Quinn, *Smokey Hollow* (1991).
78   www.overheardindublin.com, 20 August 2005.
79   Overheard on the 27 bus, 10 October 2005.
80   *The Irish Times,* 5 October 1944.
81   Raymond O'Donoghue, 'Motoring in Dublin in 1934', *Dublin Historical Record,*
      June–September 1984.
82   Andrews, op. cit.
83   *The Irish Times,* 10 May 1941.

84   Paddy Crosbie, *Your Dinner's Poured Out* (1981).
85   Denis Johnston, 'The Dublin Trams', *Dublin Historical Record,* November 1951.
86   Dominic Behan, *My Brother Brendan* (London 1965).
87   Corcoran, op.cit.
88   *The Irish Times,* 4 August 2001.
89   *My Dublin,* quoted Curriculum Development Unit, *Dublin 1913,* 1978.
90   Paddy Crosbie, op. cit.
91   Paddy Lynch, quoted in Kearns, op. cit.
92   Quoted in Kearns, op. cit.
93   Joyce, op.cit.
94   MacThomáis, op. cit.
95   O'Donoghue, op. cit.
96   Anne Simpson, *Blooming Dublin* (Edinburgh 1991).
97   *Sunday Tribune,* 12 September 2004.
98   Ross O'Carroll Kelly, *Sunday Tribune,* 26 June 2005.
99   *The Irish Times,* 18 March 2006.
100 *The Irish Times,* 7 July 2004.
101 *Sunday Tribune,* 26 June 2005.
102 *The Irish Times,* 8 February 2006
103 Eoin O'Brien, *The Beckett Country* (Dublin & London 1986).
104 Brian Mac Aongusa, *The Harcourt Street Line* (2003).
105 Simpson, op. cit.
106 *The Irish Times,* 8 November 2003.
107 Quinn, op. cit.
108 Paddy Crosbie, op. cit.
109 *The Irish Times,* 29 September 2004.
110 *Sunday Tribune,* 19 January 2003.
111 Killian Doyle, *The Irish Times,* 3 August 2005.
112 Michael O'Regan, *The Irish Times,* 10 February 2006.
113 Quoted in Kearns, op. cit.
114 'Some Old Street Characters of Dublin', *Dublin Historical Record,* December 1939/March 1940.
115 Roddy Doyle, *Brownbread* (London 1989).
116 Oliver St John Gogarty, *As I was going down Sackville Street* (London 1936).
117 *Irish Independent,* January 1981.
118 'Irishology', *The Irish Times,* 2 April 2005.
119 *The Irish Times,* April 2005.

Chapter 3: DO YOU TAKE STILUMANTS? (PP. 63–82)
1   *Sunday Tribune,* 7 June 1998.
2   Paddy Linehan, *Yesterday's Ireland* (2003).
3   Gerald P. Delahunty, 'Dialect and Local Accent', in Diarmaid Ó Muirithe (ed.), *The English Language in Ireland* (Dublin & Cork 1977).
4   *The Phoenix,* Dublin, 8 April 2005.
5   Rose Doyle, *Trade Names* (2004).
6   'Tom Lalor's Yeats Cartoon', *History Ireland,* winter 2004.
7   C.S. Andrews, *Dublin Made Me,* op. cit.
8   Samuel Beckett, *Dream of Fair to Middling Women* (1992, written 1932).
9   *The Phoenix,* 8 April 2005.
10   Richard Head, *Hic et Ubique, or The Humours of Dublin* (London 1663).
11   James Joyce, *Ulysses* (London 1937).
12   *The Irish Times,* 6 September 2003.
13   *Sunday Tribune,* 1 July 2001.
14   *The Irish Times,* 14 July 2005.
15   *Sunday Tribune,* 24 April 2005.
16   'Time for T', *The Irish Times,* 18 December 2004.

17 *The Irish Times*, 4 January 2005.
18 *Sunday Tribune*, 1 August 2004.
19 Ibid., 7 February 1999.
20 Una Gildea, *Sunday Tribune*, 1 August 2004.
21 James Beattie, *Dissertations Moral & Critical* (London 1783).
22 Quoted in Gildea, op. cit.
23 Ibid.
24 *Sunday Tribune*, 3 July 2005.
25 *Sydney Morning Herald*, 26–27 July 2003.
26 Gildea, op. cit.
27 Charles Macklin, *The True-Born Irishman* (1793).
28 See Donal O'Sullivan, 'Dublin Slang Songs, with Music'. *Dublin Historical Record*, September 1938.
29 Thomas King Moylan, 'Dublin's Debt to the House of Industry', *Dublin Historical Record*, September 1938.
30 William Makepeace Thackeray, *The Irish Sketch Book* (London 1843).
31 Tom Corkery, *Tom Corkery's Dublin* (1980).
32 P.W. Joyce, *English as We Speak in it Ireland* (1910).
33 Corkery, op.cit.
34 Éamonn MacThomáis, *Janey Mack, Me Shirt is Black*, op. cit.
35 Myles na gCopaleen, *The Irish Times*, 3 June 1949.
36 'Diary of a Dublin football fan', *Sunday Tribune*, 21 June 1998.
37 *The Irish Times*, 11 October 1993.
38 Ibid., 12 March 2005.
39 Catherine Cleary, *Sunday Tribune*, 24 July 2005.
40 Roddy Doyle, *The Woman Who Walked Into Doors* (London 1996).
41 See Francis Grose, *Classical Dictionary of the Vulgar Tongue* (London 1785).
42 Diarmuid Ó Muirithe, *The Words We Use* (1996).
43 Andrews, op. cit.
44 Seán O'Casey, *Drums Under the Windows* (London 1945).
45 Myles na gCopaleen, *The Best of Myles* (London 1968).
46 'I'm after being sick of speaking American, you guys', *Sunday Tribune*, 6 March 2003.
47 *Sunday Tribune*, 4 September 2005.
48 Beatrice Bayley Butler, 'A Dublin Tapestry; Florence Mary Evans 1887–1973', *Dublin Historical Record*, June 1976.
49 Myles na gCopaleen, *The Hair of the Dogma* (London 1977).
50 Gene Kerrigan, *Another Country, Growing up in '50s Ireland* (1998).
51 Alan Roberts, *The Rasherhouse* (Cork 1997).
52 Graham Seal, *The Lingo* (Sydney 1999).
53 'Diary of a Dublin fan', *Sunday Tribune*, 28 June 1998.
54 Seán O'Casey, *The Plough and the Stars* (London 1926).
55 Samuel Beckett, *Dream of Fair to Middling Women*, op. cit.
56 Brendan Behan, *Moving Out*, op. cit.
57 Bob Quinn, *Smokey Hollow* (1991).
58 *The Irish Times*, 18 July 1997.
59 Ibid., 9 April 2005.
60 Publican Frank Gleeson, interviewed by Rose Doyle in April 2005, rubbished the notion 'that there were ever "good old days". Standards of living now are higher, even the man doing the most menial of jobs has money in his pocket' ('Tradenames', *The Irish Times*, 13 April 2005).
61 Gildea, op. cit.
62 'No fries with that, mate', *Sydney Morning Herald*, 26–27 July 2003.

Chapter 4: Oh! My! God! (pp. 83–108)
1 *The Irish Times*, 22 November 2004.
2 William Thomson, *A Tour through Ireland in 1807* (London 1813).
3 *Sunday Tribune*, 17 July 2005.

4   Gene Kerrigan, *Another Country* (1998).
5   'The Cruise of the *Calabar*', Colm Ó Lochlainn, *More Irish Street Ballads* (1965).
6   'Just the Ticket', *The Irish Times*, 13 April 2005.
7   'Word Games', *The Irish Times*, 20 November 2004.
8   Roddy Doyle, *Brownbread* (ibid).
9   Vincent Caprani, *Vulgar Verse & Variations*, op. cit.
10 Maria and Richard Lovell Edgeworth, *An Essay on Irish Bulls* (London 1802).
11 Tom Corkery, *Tom Corkery's Dublin* (1980).
12 Gerald P. Delahunty, 'Dialect and Local Accent' in Diarmaid Ó Muirithe, ed., *The English Language in Ireland* (Dublin & Cork, 1977).
13 Éamonn MacThomáis, *The 'Labour' and the Royal* (1979).
14 *Sunday Tribune*, 20 March 2005.
15 James Joyce, *Ulysses* (London 1937).
16 *Sunday Tribune*, 1 May 2005.
17 Bob Quinn, *Smokey Hollow* (1991).
18 Paul Durcan, 'What is a Protestant, Daddy?' in *Teresa's Bar* (Oldcastle, Co. Meath, 1986).
19 Kerrigan, op. cit.
20 C.S. Andrews, *Dublin Made Me* (ibid.).
21 Dominic Behan, *Teems of Times and Happy Returns* (London 1961).
22 Leslie Daiken, *Out Goes She, Dublin street rhymes with a commentary* (1963).
23 Anne Simpson, *Blooming Dublin* (Edinburgh 1991).
24 Éamonn MacThomáis, *Janey Mack, me Shirt is Black*, op. cit.
25 James Joyce, *Dubliners* (London 1914).
26 *Word 4 Word*, BBC, 3 August 2005.
27 Vicky Howard, overheardindublin.com, 22 July 2005.
28 Caprani, op. cit.
29 *The Irish Times*, 13 October 2005.
30 Kerrigan, op. cit.
31 Daiken, op. cit.
32 *The Irish Times*, 1 November 2005.
33 Seán O'Casey, *Pictures in the Hallway* (London 1963).
34 Christy Brown, *Down All the Days* (London 1970).
35 *The Irish Times*, 17 August 2005.
36 'Word Games', *The Irish Times*, 20 November 2004.
37 Quoted in Roberta Gray, 'There's one "f" in Ireland', *Sunday Tribune*, 22 February 2004.
38 *Sunday Tribune*, 15 February 2004.
39 Gray, op. cit.
40 Paddy Crosbie, *Your Dinner's Poured Out!* (1981).
41 Jesse Sheidlower (ed.), *The F-Word*, 2nd ed. (New York 1999).
42 *Sunday Independent*, 29 August 2004.
43 Alan Roberts, *The Rasherhouse*, op. cit.
44 Gray, op. cit.
45 Argelio Santiesteban, *El Habla Popular Cubana de Hoy* (Havana 1997).
46 See Joaquim Pomares, *Diccionari del Català Popular i d'Argot* (Barcelona 1997).
47 Doyle, op. cit.
48 Gray, op. cit.
49 Kerrigan, op. cit.
50 *The Irish Times*, 1 June 2005.
51 Gray, op. cit.
52 *Sunday Tribune*, 15 February 2004.
53 Lee Dunne, *Goodbye to the Hill* (1986).
54 Quinn, op. cit.
55 Samuel Beckett, *Dream of Fair to Middling Women* (1992, written 1932).
56 Joyce, *Ulysses*, op. cit.
57 Ian O'Doherty, *Irish Independent*, 20 July 2005.
58 Roberts, op. cit.

59   Dermot Bolger, *The Journey Home* (London 1990).
60   *The Irish Times*, 7 February 2005.
61   Jonathon Green, *Cassell's Dictionary of Slang* (London 1998).
62   Roberts, op. cit.
63   Doyle, op. cit.
64 · Roberts, op. cit.
65   *Sunday Tribune*, 22 May 2005.
66   Amsterdam by Anonymous, overheardindublin.com, 29 July 2005.
67   Joan Beal, *English Pronunciation in the Eighteenth Century* (Oxford 1999).
68   Joyce, *Ulysses*, op. cit.
69   Flann O'Brien, *The Hard Life* (London 1961).
70   *The Irish Times*, 13 May 2003.
71   Éamonn MacThomáis, *Me Jewel and Darlin' Dublin* (1974).
72   James Joyce, 'Ivy Day in the Committee Room', *Dubliners* (London 1914).
73   Roddy Doyle, *Rory and Ita* (London 2002).
74   Doyle, *Brownbread*, op. cit.
75   *Sunday Tribune*, 15 May 2005.
76   Patrick Boland, *Tales from a City Farmyard* (1955).
77   *The Irish Times*, 23 March 2005.
78   *Sunday Tribune*, 22 August 2004.
79   *Irish Independent*, 6 August 2005.
80   *Sunday Tribune*, 14 August 2005.
81   'Told me in Grogans by Malcolm', overheardindublin.com, 27 July 2005.
82   O'Brien, op. cit.
83   Caprani, op. cit.
84   Myles na gCopaleen, *Nonplus*, October 1959.
85   Ibid., *The Best of Myles* (London 1968).
86   Simpson, op.cit.
87   Rosita Boland, *The Irish Times*, 29 June 2005.
88   *The Irish Times*, 7 February 2005.
89   *Cara*, July 2005.
90   *Sunday Tribune*, 28 January 1996.
91   Dermot Bolger, *Emily's Shoes* (London 1992).
92   *Sunday Tribune*, 21 September 2003.

Chapter 5: 40 PACES FROM O'CONNELL BRIDGE (PP. 109–42)
1   *The Irish Times*, 8 December 2001.
2   Ibid., 18 December 2004.
3   Ibid., 20 December 1997.
4   Ibid., 9 June 2005.
5   Araminta Wallace, ibid., 29 December 2001.
6   Roderick W. Childers, *Brendan Behan. Chicago Today III* (Chicago 1966).
7   Samuel A. Ossory Fitzpatrick, *Dublin, Historical & Topographical Account of the City* (1907).
8   Seán O'Casey, *Pictures in the Hallway* (London 1963).
9   Éamonn MacThomáis, *Janey Mack, me Shirt is Black*, op. cit.
10   *Dublin Chamber of Commerce Year Book*, 1917.
11   Ibid.
12   Kieran Hickey, *Faithful Departed* (1982).
13   Bob Quinn, *Smokey Hollow* (1991).
14   *The Irish Times*, 14 May 1999.
15   Quinn, op. cit.
16   Hugh Oram, *The Advertising Book* (1986).
17   Moira Lysaght, 'My Dublin', *Dublin Historical Record*, September 1977.
18   James Joyce, 'A Painful Case', *Dubliners* (London 1914).
19   Éamonn MacThomáis, *Me Jewel and Darlin' Dublin*, op. cit.
20   Brendan Behan, *Richard's Cork Leg*, op. cit.

21   12 October 1945. Quoted in *History Ireland*, Summer 2004.
22   Quinn, op. cit.
23   *Sunday Tribune*, 11 September 2005.
24   Maria and Richard Lovell Edgeworth, *An Essay on Irish Bulls*, op. cit.
25   Raymond Queneau, *Les Oeuvres Complètes de Sally Mara* (Paris 1950).
26   Jonathan Swift, *The Drapier's Letters* (1724).
27   Jonathon Green, *Cassell's Dictionary of Slang* (London 1998).
28   *Dublin Evening Post*, 5 January 1826.
29   O'Casey, op. cit.
30   Ibid.
31   Letter to the author, 6 February 1997.
32   James Joyce, *Ulysses* (London 1937).
33   Anon, *The Irish Times*, 23 June 2005.
34   Samuel Beckett, *More Pricks than Kicks* (London 1934).
35   Seán O'Casey, *Juno and the Paycock* (London 1924).
36   *The Irish Times*, 15 November 2003.
37   Tom Corkery, *Tom Corkery's Dublin*, op. cit.
38   Ibid.
39   Ibid.
40   Arthur Hall, trade union regional secretary, quoted in *The Irish Times*, 12 August 2005.
41   Roddy Doyle, *The Woman who Walked into Doors* (London 1996).
42   Roddy Doyle, ibid.
43   Stephen, overheardindublin.com, 2 September 2005.
44   Gene Kerrigan, *Another Country* (1998).
45   Tom Corkery, op. cit.
46   Christy Brown, *Down All the Days* (London 1970).
47   Roddy Doyle, *Rory and Ita* (London 2002).
48   *The Irish Times*, 11 September 2001.
49   *Sunday Tribune*, 30 December 2001.
50   *The Irish Times*, 16 December 2002.
51   www.overheardindublin.com, 20 April 2005.
52   Louis MacNeice, *Autumn Journal* (London 1939).
53   Jonah Barrington, *Personal Sketches* (London 1827/32).
54   Vincent Caprani, *A View from the DART* (Dublin, 1986).
55   Peadar Kearney, *Fish and Chips*, quoted in Colm Ó Lochlainn, *More Irish Street Ballads* (1965).
56   Rosita Boland, 'House of Hutchinson, House of Murphy' in *Dublin Review*, spring 2005.
57   Éamonn MacThomáis, *The 'Labour' and the Royal* (1979).
58   O'Casey, Pictures in the Hallway, op. cit.
59   Samuel Beckett, *Dream of Fair to Middling Women* (ibid).
60   Éamonn MacThomáis, *The 'Labour' & the Royal*, op. cit.
61   Theodora Fitzgibbon, *Irish Traditional Food* (Dublin, 1983).
62   Siobhán O'Connor, *Sunday Independent*, 17 July 2005.
63   Orna Mulcahy, *The Irish Times*, 24 July 2004.
64   Theodora Fitzgibbon, op. cit.
65   *Sunday Independent*, 22 August 1999.
66   Samuel Beckett, *Dream of Fair to Middling Women*, op. cit.
67   Corkery, op. cit.
68   *Sunday Tribune*, 30 October 2004.
69   Myles na gCopaleen, *The Best of Myles* (London 1968).
70   Roisín Ingle, *The Irish Times*, 5 February 2005.
71   RTÉ radio programme, *Get the Pint*, 9 July 1999.
72   Joyce, *Ulysses*, op. cit.
73   Ibid., *Finnegans Wake* (London 1939).
74   Flann O'Brien, *At Swim-Two-Birds* (London 1939).
75   Headline, *Sunday Tribune*, 29 May 2005.

76 James Joyce, *Dubliners*, op. cit.
77 Beckett, *Dream of Fair to Middling Women*, op. cit.
78 Diarmuid Doyle, *Sunday Tribune*, 24 April 2005.
79 Deaglán de Bréadún, *The Irish Times*, 21 August 2004.
80 Roddy Doyle, *Rory and Ita*, op. cit.
81 Oliver St John Gogarty, *It Isn't This Time Of Year At All!* (London 1954).
82 Dermot Bolger, *Emily's Shoes* (London 1992).
83 John Clement Ryan, *Irish Whiskey* (1992).
84 Beckett, *More Pricks than Kicks*, op. cit.
85 Theodora Fitzgibbon, op. cit.
86 *The Irish Times*, 13 September 2005.
87 Op. cit, 8 April 2004.
88 Corkery, op. cit.
89 *Sunday Tribune*, 12 February 2006.
90 Ulick O'Connor, *The Bailey. The Story of a Famous Tavern* (1968).
91 *Sunday Tribune*, 14 July 2005.
92 *The Irish Times*, 27 March 2004.
93 'Do You Speak Irish?', *Cara*, July 2005.
94 Myles na gCopaleen, *The Best of Myles*, op. cit.
95 *Sunday Tribune*, 1 January 2003.
96 Manuel Lechado García, *Diccionario de Eufemismos* (Madrid 2000).
97 Ross Golden-Bannon, op. cit.
98 Myles na gCopaleen, *The Best of Myles*, op. cit.
99 Ross O'Carroll Kelly, *Sunday Tribune*, 13 June 2004.
100 Ibid., 4 September 2005.
101 James Plunkett, 'Finegan's Ark', *Collected Short Stories* (Swords 1977).
102 Gerry O'Malley, *The Irish Times*, 19 July 2001.
103 Quoted *Sunday Tribune*, 21 November 2004.
104 Jonathon Green, op. cit.
105 Dermot Bolger, *The Journey Home* (London 1990).
106 *The Irish Times*, 13 June 2005.
107 Ulick O'Connor, op. cit.
108 *Sunday Tribune*, 22 August 2004.

Chapter 6: LAMENT FOR MOUSEY RYAN (PP. 143–71)
1 R.M. Levey and J. O'Rorke, *Annals of the Theatre Royal, Dublin* (1880).
2 Constantia Maxwell, *Dublin Under the Georges* (London 1961).
3 Ibid.
4 Levey and O'Rorke, op. cit.
5 Samuel A. Ossory Fitzpatrick, *Dublin, A Historical and Topographical Account of the City* (ibid.).
6 John Edwin, *Eccentricities* (London 1791).
7 Levey and O'Rorke, op. cit.
8 *The Irish Times*, 22 June 2005.
9 *Cara*, March/April 1988.
10 C.S. Andrews, *Dublin Made Me.*, op. cit.
11 Paddy Crosbie, *Your Dinner's Poured Out*, op. cit.
12 Gus Smith, *Eamonn Andrews, His Life* (London 1988).
13 Toby Barnard, *A New Anatomy of Ireland* (London 2003).
14 Éamonn MacThomáis, *Janey Mack, me Shirt is Black*, op. cit.
15 Joseph V. O'Brien, *'Dear, Dirty Dublin', a City in Distress 1899–1916* (Berkeley 1992).
16 Peter Somerville-Large, *Dublin* (London 1979).
17 Seán O'Casey, *Pictures in the Hallway* (London 1963).
18 *The Irish Times*, 7 March 1959.
19 Johnson's original is *nullum quod tetegit non ornavit*: he touched nothing that he did not adorn.
20 *The Irish Times*, 18 October 1939.

21   Progressive Democrats.
22   *Sunday Business Post*, 31 July 2005.
23   'My Dublin', *Dublin Historical Record*, September 1977.
24   Andrews, op. cit.
25   Crosbie, op. cit.
26   Éamonn MacThomáis, *Me Jewel and Darlin' Dublin*, op. cit.
27   Leslie Daiken, *Out Goes She* (1963).
28   Dominic Behan, *My Brother Brendan*, op. cit.
29   Crosbie, op. cit.
30   MacThomáis, *Me Jewel and Darlin' Dublin*, op. cit.
31   O'Casey, op. cit.
32   Kevin C. Kearns, *Dublin Street Life and Lore* (1991).
33   Dermot Bolger, *Emily's Shoes*, op. cit.
34   MacThomáis, *Me Jewel and Darlin' Dublin*, op. cit.
35   Jonah Barrington, *Personal Sketches* (London 1827/32).
36   Tom Humphries, *The Irish Times*, 4 July 2005.
37   *The Irish Times*, 22 November 2003.
38   Jason Burt, *Independent on Sunday*, London, 20 March 2005.
39   *Sunday Tribune*, 17 April 2005.
40   *The Irish Times*, 3 December 2005.
41   Dáil Reports, 1922-3.
42   Michael Clifford, *Sunday Tribune*, 24 July 2005.
43   Tom Corkery, *Tom Corkery's Dublin* (ibid.).
44   *Sunday Tribune*, 21 August 2005.
45   Barrington, op. cit.
46   Contemporary ballad.
47   Ossory Fitzpatrick, op. cit.
48   Somerville-Large, op.cit.
49   Maria and Richard Lovell Edgeworth, *An Essay on Irish Bulls*, op. cit.
50   'Dublin Slang Songs, with music', *Dublin Historical Record*, September 1938.
51   Tim Carey, *Mountjoy – the Story of a Prison* (Cork 2000).
52   Quoted in Carey, op. cit.
53   *I Did Penal Servitude* (1945).
54   *Irish Press*, 21 May 1964.
55   Donal MacCarron, *Step Together* (1999).
56   Alan Roberts, *The Rasherhouse*, op. cit.
57   *Sunday Tribune*, 10 April 2005.
58   Ibid., 6 March 2005.
59   Bill Kelly, *Me Darlin' Dublin's Dead & Gone* (1983).
60   Jim Phelan, quoted in Curriculum Development Unit, *Dublin 1913 – a Divided City* (1982).
61   *The Irish Times*, 28 August 1913.
62   Moira Lysaght, 'My Dublin', *Dublin Historical Record*, September 1977.
63   Andrews, op. cit.
64   Timothy Dawson, 'Of Cooks and Coffin Makers', *Dublin Historical Record*, June 1977.
65   Toby Barnard, *A New Anatomy of Ireland* (London 2003).
66   *Yes, Taoiseach*, Dubllin 2004.
67   Dawson, op. cit.
68   Éamonn MacThomáis, *The 'Labour' and the Royal*, op. cit.
69   Willie Murphy, quoted in Kevin C. Kearns, *Dublin Street Life & Lore* (1991).
70   Ibid.
71   Ibid.
72   Vincent Caprani, *A Whang of Slang* (1989).
73   Ibid.
74   James Joyce, *Dubliners* (London 1914).
75   O'Casey, op. cit.
76   Roddy Doyle, *Rory & Ita* (London 2002).

77 Paddy Linehan, *Yesterday's Ireland* (ibid.).
78 Peter Somerville-Large, *Irish Voices* (London 1999).
79 Joseph V. O'Brien, '*Dear, Dirty Dublin*' (Berkeley and Los Angeles, 1982).
80 Ibid.
81 'Ghosts of Old Dublin', *Dublin Historical Record*, December 1976.
82 John Ryan, *Remembering How We Stood* (1975).
83 O'Casey, op. cit.
84 Dominic Behan, *Teems of Times and Happy Returns*, op. cit.
85 James Joyce, *Ulysses* (London 1936).
86 Mary Jones, *These Obstreperous Lassies, a History of the Irish Women Workers' Union* (1988).
87 Ibid.

Chapter 7: Pigeon English (pp. 172–85)
 1 *The Irish Times*, 8 January 2005.
 2 William Reville, *The Irish Times*, 1 September 2005.
 3 *Sunday Tribune*, 26 June 2005.
 4 *Independent on Sunday* (London), 2 October 2005.
 5 *The Irish Times*, 10 May 2005.
 6 Ibid., 12 August 2005.
 7 Don Watson, *Gobbledygook* (London 2005).
 8 *Irish Independent*, 13 August 2005.
 9 *The Irish Times*, 4 October 2005.
10 *Irish Independent*, 27 August 2005.
11 *The Irish Times*, 27 August 2005.
12 Ibid., 13 June 2005.
13 David Crystal, *The Cambridge Encyclopaedia of the English Language* (Cambridge 1995).
14 *The Irish Times*, 18 December 2004.
15 Ibid., 28 September 2005.
16 Ibid., 4 October 2005.
17 Ibid., 13 June 2005.
18 *Sunday Tribune*, 19 June 2005.
19 Thomas Naghten, *The Irish Times*, 26 November 2004.
20 *The Irish Times*, 16 August 2005.
21 Ibid., 4 December 2004.
22 Ibid., 16 August 2005.
23 Ibid., 16 July 2005.
24 *History Ireland*, May/June 2005.
25 Ibid., September/October 2005.
26 Ibid.
27 Paddy Crosbie, *Your Dinner's Poured Out!*, op. cit.
28 *The Irish Times*, 27 August 2005.
29 Nino Culotta, *They're a Weird Mob* (Sydney 1957).
30 Anon, *The Irish Times*, 18 August 2005.
31 Quoted in Graham Seal, *The Lingo* (Sydney 1999).
32 *The Irish Times*, 2 February 2005.

INDEX